# EVERYBODY PAYS A VIG

*One Man's Entrepreneurial Journey*

Craig Sotkovsky

Copyright 2018 by Craig Sotkovsky.

All rights reserved. Published in the United States of America. Except as permitted under the United States Copyright Act of 1976, no part of this publication may be reproduced or distributed in any form or by any means, or stored in a database or retrieval system, without the prior written permission of the publisher.

This book is presented solely for educational, motivational and entertainment purposes. It is a literary work. It is not offered as legal, accounting, tax, or other professional services advice. It is not intended to take the place of legal, accounting, or financial advisors. This book is a work of creative effort and reflects the author's recollection of experiences over time and the conversations reflected herein are the author's recollections and interpretations. They are not intended as a verbatim transcript. To protect privacy, some names and events have been changed, modified, or created. The opinions expressed by the author are his personal opinions and he is not responsible for any use of such opinions or reliance thereon.

Photography by Nishi Sotkovsky.
Edited by Monique Huenergardt
Published by 2920 LLC

ISBN: 978-1-7322324-1-9

*Dedicated to my wife and daughter who inspire
me to be a better human…95% of the time.*

MERRIAM-WEBSTER DEFINITION

vig·or·ish

ˈvigəriSH/

*noun*

*U.S. informal*

1.  an excessive rate of interest on a loan, typically one from an illegal moneylender.
2.  the percentage deducted from a gambler's winnings by the organizers of a game.

CRAIG'S DEFINITION

vig

*noun*

*U.S. informal*

1.  a tax you pay on every transaction in your life, financial or otherwise, that you never get back (unless you become the House).

# CONTENTS

Prologue ............................................................................................................1
Chapter 1 ..........................................................................................................3
Chapter 2 ........................................................................................................21
Chapter 3 ........................................................................................................37
Chapter 4 ........................................................................................................50
Chapter 5 ........................................................................................................70
Chapter 6 ........................................................................................................91
Chapter 7 ......................................................................................................108
Chapter 8 ......................................................................................................118
Chapter 9 ......................................................................................................134
Chapter 10 ....................................................................................................150
Chapter 11 ....................................................................................................163
A Mexican Epilogue ....................................................................................183

# PROLOGUE

**January 20, 2009**
**George Bush Intercontinental Airport, Houston, Texas**

With the inaugural speech looping on televisions in the background, we rushed through the airport to our gate. My wife pushed our daughter in the stroller while I carried our backpacks and the diaper bag. I kept hearing "change, change, change," and I thought to myself, "The only thing we have left is change." The system had already stolen our goddamned dollars. We were making our own big change and starting a new life.

I think I was traumatized, by the attacks of 9/11, by the hurricanes and their aftermath, and by my failed attempt to teach financial literacy to the masses. But mostly, I was traumatized by the realization that the country I was born and raised in had been taken over by banks and was now completely screwed. At this point, I didn't care. I was worn out, burned out, depressed, and I didn't know which way was up.

There was no turning back. There was no more credit, no more mortgage money, and no way to dig ourselves out. We walked away from our home and left my Nissan Titan in the driveway. I sent the keys to our second house to the bank and sold the office for a fifth of what we'd paid for it. Man, what a nightmare! But what else could we do?

For me, it was a no-brainer. Staying would have meant working day and night to repair all the holes in our sinking ship, being stressed out all the time, and missing our daughter growing up. Somehow, I'd gotten into the position of chasing currency instead of chasing my dream and ended up facing a vig much larger than we were prepared to pay. We were starting a new life, this time walking our own path instead of traveling the one laid out for us. Like George Carlin said, "It's the American Dream, because you have to be asleep to believe it."

In so many ways, we all end up paying the vig along our personal journey through life. Not just financially, but in sacrificed relationships, lost time, and deteriorating health and happiness. I don't know where it all went wrong. Maybe I have to go back to the beginning, to how it all started when, as a kid in New Jersey, I learned that everything in life has a price.

# CHAPTER 1

## Growing Up in Jersey

**The Early Years**

I was born in Jersey City, New Jersey in 1965 to a blue-collar working-class family. My father, Bob, drove a tractor-trailer making deliveries throughout New York City and the outer boroughs. My mother, Lorraine, worked at a bank for many years in addition to raising three kids. I'm the youngest. My brother, Mark, is three years older, and my sister, Vicki, is twelve years older.

  The family story of my entry into the world has stuck with me quite profoundly. My grandmother Mary was dying, and my mother went to visit her in the hospital. This was before doctors used ultrasound to determine a baby's gender, but my grandmother told her daughter she was carrying a beautiful baby boy. Grandma passed away that evening, and I was born the next morning in the same hospital. I guess sometimes when one soul leaves, it's replaced by another.

During my earliest years, we lived in a two-story walk-up on the corner of Kamp Place and New York Avenue in North Bergen. Our three-bedroom cold-water flat was on the second floor, and we shared the only bathroom with the tenant across the hall. He was a big guy who kind of scared Mark and me, so we often found creative ways to avoid using that bathroom at night. We thought we were so clever pretending it was the radiator leaking, but Mom knew better.

Our backyard was Hudson County Park: 167 acres including baseball fields, a football field, the sixteen-acre Woodcliff Lake, a stream, and a playground. Our neighborhood was a mix of Irish, German, Italian, Polish, and Slav. Everybody got along like one big family, and I called most of the adults "aunt" and "uncle." We all traipsed through each other's houses as if they were our own and got yelled at by the other parents as if we were their own. On warm, star-filled nights, all the families gathered on each other's porches and ate supper together. Afterward, the kids played in the street while the adults sat around drinking and laughing.

Before I was old enough to go to school, Mom used to take me on the bus to Journal Square to spend the day. She went to the gym above Woolworth's, and while she was sweating to the oldies, I was downstairs ordering a grilled cheese sandwich. While I ate my sandwich at the counter, I watched all the people coming and going. I had a perfect view out onto the street and watched and listened to the cars, buses, trucks, police, and fire engines race by. I watched vendors selling fruit from their sidewalk stands and wondered if their kids missed their fathers as much as I missed mine. It was a little kid's wonderland and my early introduction to the hustle and bustle of street life. I thought I was so independent, sitting at the counter by myself with my sandwich. Years later I found out the lady at the counter was my mom's friend and she was watching me while my mother was at the gym.

Summers meant playing at the town pool. All the kids in the neighborhood spent the day there until the dads arrived after work. Families gathered around the tables by the concession stand, and orders of hamburgers and hot dogs came fast and heavy. Every afternoon, Mark and I waited by the fence for Dad to pull his truck into the warehouse yard next door. I saw how tired he was, but he always played with us in the pool. I think it relaxed him after a hard day and getting tossed around in the pool was a bonus for us.

## Learning About Work

I always asked my dad about his day, where he went, what he carried on his truck and, most important to me, when I'd be able to go to work with him. At first he laughed, probably thinking a little kid had no business on a truck. But I was relentless and never stopped asking when I could go with him. Finally, he told me I could come along after my fifth birthday. I counted down the days, and on my birthday, I didn't care about presents or cake. All I wanted was to be on a truck with my dad because he treated me like a grownup.

Dad was strong and encouraged his kids to be strong. Being a former Marine, he had no time for tears, and he made sure we didn't either. Whatever went down, we had to suck it up and move on. We were spoiled with love, not material things. He worked hard, and he thought we should, too. He was my hero.

I remember looking at my dad's rig the first day I went to work with him. The cab was filled with gadgets and numbers and switches—it looked like a cockpit to me—and it was HUGE. Several feet off the ground, it almost felt like I was in the clouds looking down at the world.

Dad taught me the importance of responsibility and punctuality. Every morning was the same routine. We checked the tractor and its fluids, hooked up the trailer, then checked the air lines, tires, tail lights, directional lights, and air brakes, which popped and hissed when they were connected. He showed me the manifests and explained what we were carrying, where we had to go, and what time we had to be there. Now, instead of watching the world through Woolworth's window, I was part of it.

We delivered to stores and to the docks in Manhattan, Queens, the Bronx, Brooklyn, and Long Island. The manifest listed every box and which stop it needed to go to, and every box was numbered accordingly. When we got to a loading dock, Dad sent me into the trailer to pull out the cartons with the right numbers on them.

This is when I learned about how other people's laziness can affect my family and me. The guys who loaded the trailer knew that the boxes with a "one" on them had to be unloaded first, so should be the last ones put on the trailer. They didn't give a shit because they wouldn't be unloading, so sometimes they just shoved everything in in no particular order. Those were the times I had to climb over boxes and dig around to find the right ones and throw them out to my dad.

Everything had to run like clockwork. If there was too much traffic or the guys who loaded the truck that day were being lazy, we'd arrive at the dock late and there'd be a line of trucks waiting to unload. At times like these, all we could do was twiddle our thumbs and talk, but that was priceless uninterrupted time with my dad.

He also worked as a bouncer on the weekends. It suited him, and even though he was older than the other bouncers, they respected him as a tough son-of-a-gun. They all knew he fought in the Korean War operating a flamethrower and was one of the "Chosin Few."

I'm glad I had the opportunity to spend so much time with my dad. Working with him taught me about making a living through hard work, a lesson that's served me well throughout my life.

\* \* \*

## Pushing Boundaries and Savoring Moments

When I started kindergarten at Robert Fulton School, I couldn't go to work with Dad anymore. My life went from great to shit almost overnight. I despised sitting in a chair all day when what I wanted to do was be in the truck with my dad. I didn't like the uniforms, rules and regulations, and forced conformity. But I still managed to make friends. After school, we climbed trees, played manhunt, handball, and Cowboys and Indians, and with my friends' help, I perfected the art of making bows and arrows from twigs and branches.

According to our parents, the boundary for our wanderings was our block. But as long as we were home by suppertime, we felt free to roam a larger territory that included Hudson County Park and the church parking lot a block over. If one of our friends heard our parents calling for us, the message got relayed from kid to kid until it reached us.

Every now and again when I felt ambitious and had a dollar, I found myself at Moon Station, one of the coolest stores a kid could find. The walls were covered with fluorescent posters of peace signs, tigers, and rock stars, and the ceiling was painted black with glowing stars attached and plastic planets hanging down. It was a hippy den filled with the aroma of incense and had everything a boy could want to buy. Bags of rocks that exploded when you threw them, magic light-up snakes, vampire fangs and makeup, card tricks, and model cars. Mom usually figured out I'd gone past the boundaries when she found the gadgets in my pocket on laundry day. Despite the resulting smacks on the ass, I kept going back for the thrill of overstepping my boundaries.

On hot summer days, another favorite spot was the soda shop. Sweating from head to toe from playing and running around, I'd hop up on one of the red leather barstools at the long marble-topped counter, set my foot on the brass footrest, and order a vanilla Coke. With its black-and-white tiled floor, large mirrors, and grimy engraved tin ceiling, it was like a mob hangout.

I loved watching the Coke syrup drizzle into the glass, followed by a couple pumps of vanilla, then the glass filling with carbonated water. It fizzed and popped into the air with a hiss. I'll never forget the taste and savoring that soda before heading back out to the streets. This was my early introduction to "smelling the roses," stopping the chaos for a moment, sitting back and appreciating something as simple as a cold soda.

Some of my favorite times were spent walking with my grandfather Jack. On holidays, he would get some of the best jelly donuts and warm crumb cakes from the bakery next door to his house and walk the mile from his apartment to ours. Gramps loved to walk and alternated taking Vicki, Mark, and me. I walked with him for hours, and he told me about the old days when he was a professional boxer in the whiskey halls, and the time he almost lost his arm in an accident at a barrel company. He regaled me with stories of growing up in Ohio after his family emigrated from Czechoslovakia and how much fun it was raising my dad in West New York.

**A Big Move**

By the summer before third grade, my dad had managed to save up enough money to buy a house on Washington Place in Cliffside Park. Having our own house all to ourselves was a huge deal. It was a two-story block-construction handyman special with three bedrooms, one bathroom, a recreation room, a utility room in the basement, and a fenced-in backyard with a pool. My parents had one room, Vicki had her room, and Mark and I shared the third room.

Our former neighbors in North Bergen literally moved us into the new house, and the first order of business was clean up and repairs. Dad figured his two boys would be perfect helpers, but Mark and I had other priorities. Rolling up our sleeves and getting to work took a back seat to meeting the kids who lived on the block. Mark managed to sneak out of working most of the time, and I got out of it often enough. There were lots of kids to get to know, and we quickly befriended most of them. We traded our old backyard, Hudson County Park, for the cliffs overlooking the Hudson River, and spent the summer playing stickball, manhunt, football, and soccer. Once I started at my new school, I quickly became one of a tight group of five who were regularly sent to the principal's office for various offenses.

We all took shortcuts to school, most of which involved hopping the neighbors' fences. We had to jump two fences to get to my Italian friend's house, and we occasionally got to eat breakfast there. This was great for three reasons. First, they all spoke Italian, and although I wanted to learn Italian from my aunts and uncles, that was something I never accomplished. Second, well, free homemade breakfast. We ate whatever was left over from the night before, or his mom made eggs and potatoes. Third, and really most important, breakfast in this family was always served with a glass of homemade wine. On these mornings, we got buzzed and found ourselves getting to school a little late.

Sometimes our fence-jumping got us into trouble. There was an Italian guy who lived across the street from the school.

One day he spotted us running through his backyard and came out of the house screaming. We scaled his high fence and climbed onto his garage roof. From there, we had to jump a few feet to his neighbor's garage. By the time the old man got over to us, only one of us was still on top of his garage. He threatened our friend with a pitchfork, yelling, "Here, leta me helpa you down, you summuna bitch." The rest of us distracted the old man long enough for our buddy to hop to the next roof, and in a split second, we all tore ass down the street. Later, after the man complained to the school, we found out we'd trampled through the garden he'd just seeded. I guess sometimes karma is a bitch because it was years before I could grow a good Jersey beefsteak tomato.

    We were juvenile delinquents. And sometimes it was just plain stupidity that got us into trouble. My Italian friend's mom raised chickens in her backyard, and sometimes she'd send us to the butcher to have the birds killed and dressed. She put them in a big, thick paper bag with the ends rolled down, and we'd play kick-the-bag all the way to the butcher shop. One time we played a little too hard. When the butcher opened the bag, he said, "Wadda da fuck, da chickens are amorte!" I was sad about it until I remembered they were going to die anyway. We were more careful the next time we walked the chickens to their deaths.

## Going into Business and Money in the Bank

It was inevitable that I'd develop a hunger for making money once I realized I could have a lot more fun with a couple of bucks in my pocket that didn't come from Mom or Dad. Mark had a friend who let me help make collections on his paper route. He was one of my early mentors, showing me the ropes of hustling to make money. But delivering newspapers at some ungodly hour of the morning was definitely not for me, so I found other ways to earn some cash. I sold chocolate door-to-door, had a lemonade stand, and on Halloween my buddy and I made a haunted house in his backyard and charged ten cents per head.

The Bicentennial Independence Day in 1976 presented a unique business opportunity. The adults all talked about the thousands of people who would come to see the ships on the Hudson River during the celebration, and how much prices would increase. I was ten years old and decided to cash in on the July 4th celebration just like the adults were. It was my first big venture, and it would take skill, cunning, and finesse. I thought I had all three, and that was all it would take.

New Jersey is always hot and humid in the summer, and people will drink just about anything as long as it's cold. I "borrowed" a supermarket carriage, lined it with plywood and a pool liner I'd found down on the cliffs, and turned it into a cooler on wheels. I planned to fill it with ice and as many sodas as it would hold and sell them to the thirsty crowds on the streets overlooking the river. I made a deal with a deli owner a few blocks over that I wouldn't sell my sodas near his store, and he agreed to sell me some block ice on credit. I bought five cases of store brand soda for fifteen cents a can and decided I'd charge a premium of thirty cents just because I could.

After all the planning, deal making, and stressing, July 4th finally arrived. Ships lined the Hudson River from Jersey City and Bayonne all the way up to the George Washington Bridge in Fort Lee, and Cliffside Park had a beautiful view of everything. With the buildings and skyscrapers in the background and the battleships glistening in the water under the sun, it was quite an impressive sight. I particularly liked the old ships with huge sails flapping in the breeze, just like pirate ships.

I took my soda-filled carriage to the deli to get my ice, and quickly realized the flaw in my plan. The cart was heavy enough with just the soda and ice, but the plywood turned out to be an unnecessary additional weight. I got a friend to help me push the carriage for a vig, and we were off and running. It wasn't even noon when we sold out. After paying my overhead expenses, I put about ten dollars in my pocket. I was really proud of that, and it was the first time I experienced the adrenaline rush of a successful business deal.

At that time, my mom worked as a teller at a Savings and Loan. Between all my saved nickels and dimes, my entrepreneurial ventures, and birthday and communion money, I managed to save $100. Mom opened a savings account for me, so I could deposit the money. She was so proud when she opened my passbook to look at it that night, but the look on her face told me something was screwed up. The teller had entered $1,000,000 instead of $100. I asked her what the big deal was, and she explained that I could go to another branch of the bank and withdraw money that wasn't mine, and that would be stealing.

We went back to the bank the next day to correct the deposit. I figured they could just cross out the million and enter the hundred and that would be that. But there was a lot of yelling and finger-pointing going on, and it seemed to take hours to get the deposit fixed. That's when I realized that if some little mistake couldn't be corrected as fast as it was made, there was a bigger bullshit story behind the scenes. I learned that banks can cook their books. There's no way they could have balanced their accounts the night before, but somehow, they did something to make it look like they did.

※ ※ ※

## Fear, Death, and Abuse

My childhood wasn't all good times, running wild, and making cash. There were times of sadness and darkness, too. My mom's sister Cookie was in an institution in Secaucus, and we would all go see her as a family.

While the adults visited, we kids explored the fence-enclosed grounds. One day, I came upon an old man hunched over, crouching in the corner of a stairwell. He looked at me, cackled, and rasped, "Hey kid, got a cigarette? Pttt, pttt, pttt." I was scared shitless and blindly ran in no particular direction to put as much space as I could between that scary old man and me. I'm sure my parents didn't realize the long-term effects of taking me to a place like that would have on me. I can still hear the clanging of the old institutional doors mixed with the yelling and screaming of patients, and that old man still visits me in my dreams.

One of the biggest lessons of childhood was learning how to handle emotional events, and for me, that included living through the deaths of people close to me. One of my cousins lost control of his van on a rainy night and hit a tree. We'd gone to wakes before, but this one was different because it was for a kid. The wails were loud, the tears were heavy, the hugs were tight, and the kisses were frequent. The men performed their solemn ritual of grief gathered quietly in one corner. My aunt, his mother, died a few years later after a short battle with cancer. Some believed that she never got over losing her son and died of a broken heart.

Another memorable loss was my Uncle Jimmy. I didn't know him well, but I spent a lot of time with his wife, Kitty. She was a small, thin Sicilian woman who didn't put up with anyone's shit. She taught me to cook. Every time I visited, she'd grab my cheeks and say "Faccia bella, faccia brutta," smack my face, and then kiss me. When Dad brought her to our house from the hospital after Jimmy had just died, I looked out the window feeling helpless and sad as he helped her up the stairs. When she saw me, she just kissed me. I don't think she had the heart to pinch and smack me.

We lost another cousin in a plane crash that we'd seen on the news. He was such a great guy, taking time to play with his younger cousins whenever we went to his house. He always came up with some crazy thing to scare the shit out of us, like walking through the woods in his backyard wearing a white sheet and acting like a ghost. Or he would hide things up in the trees and drop them on us when we walked by. It could be anything, from a mannequin dressed as a scarecrow, to shoes.

At that time, I didn't understand death. I just knew that someone wasn't coming home to their family. But I think those earlier experiences prepared me for my teen years. In middle school, one of my buddies died in a motocross crash. Later a girl I knew in school drowned in the reservoir where many of us swam and hung out.

Although kids usually bounce back after a death and life gets back to normal, some things leave a deep scar that never completely heals. When I was ten years old, my life changed abruptly one dark day, and I went from being innocent and carefree to feeling scared and dead inside. I was dragged into the twisted world of a seedy neighborhood character, and it was something I never saw coming.

Like most skilled predators, he was charming, saying the right things, acting appropriately in social settings, and ingratiating himself with the adults by running errands for them. He built up trust with the neighborhood families, a trust that he violated when he got one of us alone. I thought I was the only one. He convinced me I had done something wrong and threatened to hurt my family if I said anything. I found out there were other kids on his radar, and that I'd gotten off easier than some. I was bigger than most and could push him away. Most of the time.

I was disgusted with myself and afraid my family would be mad at me. I wondered what I had done wrong to have such a monster in my life. I was just a kid and didn't know who to turn to. He was good at cornering kids and getting us alone, and we got really freaked out whenever we saw him in the street. We coped by smoking weed and cigarettes at a friend's house or climbing down the cliffs to forget the shit running through our heads. But that didn't always work. I got into fights often just so I could feel something instead of the constant numbness inside. I lost most of those fights because I usually picked bigger kids.

Soon I looked for another outlet because fighting wasn't all that productive. Walking and baseball became my therapy, my first taste of healing from emotional trauma. I thought about my grandfather as I walked the mile to and from the field and used baseball as a way to come back to life. It was a lot of fun and I was a natural. Baseball season found me spending less time wandering the cliffs and more time on the field. Marching in local parades wearing my uniform, I couldn't have been prouder and wondered if this was what it was like to be a New York Yankee.

I met one of my best friends, Larry, on the ball field. He was a spunky kid who played shortstop and second base, while I played first base. We practiced together on and off the field and got better as a duo. Soon we dominated games and played on the city's all-star team just about every year.

I had a heavy swing for my age. During one all-star tournament, we played against the neighboring town in the finals. Their pitcher was a big Puerto Rican kid with an extreme fastball. At the bottom of the seventh inning, the score was still 0-0. I'd already struck out twice and was getting frustrated. At my last at-bat, I swung and missed a couple of pitches before I connected and blasted his fastball over the fence. My dad couldn't make it to all my games because of work, but he was there that day. His cheering me on as we won the tournament 1-0 made the win that much sweeter. A proud day, indeed.

\*\*\*

## A Mentor and Turning Points

In middle school, I met one of my early mentors, my math teacher Mr. Phillips. He was incredibly intelligent, always impeccably dressed, and had the greatest sense of humor. I was never good at math and didn't think I'd need to use such complicated concepts. But he had a different style of teaching, equating mathematical concepts to real-life scenarios. Even though I wasn't the best student, or even an average student, he never made me feel stupid or useless. He wasn't just a teacher, he was also a friend.

While I'm sorry to say I don't remember the math lessons, I clearly remember the empathy and love he had for his students. He always asked how we were doing and took a genuine interest in our lives. I felt comfortable enough to talk to him about almost anything, and he gave me a sense of worth when I sorely needed it.

During that time, there was nothing better than going to the sports store owned by one of my dad's friends. When we walked in, we had carte blanche on anything we needed or wanted. One day after we'd had our usual visit, we drove home through West New York. We were stopped at a traffic light and got rear-ended. The car wasn't badly damaged, and Mom was the only one hurt, though not terribly, so we went home after the accident. But after a few days of severe pain, she went to the hospital and we discovered there was a lot of soft tissue damage in her neck and back. She never fully recovered from the accident, and that injury contributed to her declining health until she died years later.

The summer after I graduated from middle school, my life took another turn, one that would follow me into adulthood. I was playing for the town baseball league, and the team sometimes got to the field early to warm up. That particular day, I was wearing brand-new cleats, and I hadn't worn them in properly. I decided to lead off practice by hitting a pitch out of the park. That pitch turned out to be one of those moments that felt like time had slowed.

I swung the bat and extended my left leg, my entire body moving with the swing. But my right foot, in its brand-new cleat, stayed firmly anchored in the ground. Everyone heard the POP and rushed over to me as I fell to the ground screaming in pain. There were no adults there yet, so I had to wait until our coach arrived to get a ride home. I'd had my share of bumps, bruises, broken bones, and scars, but this was very different. By the time I got home, my knee had swollen to the size of a football.

Mom packed my leg with ice and took me to the doctor's office by taxi. After what seemed like hours in the waiting room, I got x-rays of my leg. I was in excruciating pain when the doctor told me I would feel much better once my knee was "drained." I had no idea what that meant. When he pulled out a syringe that looked like the Empire State Building's radio tower, I nearly passed out. When he jabbed it into my knee and twisted it around, I blacked out.

I was going to need surgery and was sent home with some pain medication. I was clumsy on the crutches and kept hitting my foot going up the stairs, sending new waves of pain through my knee. Sitting on the couch with my leg elevated and packed with ice, I would have done anything for some relief from the pain. When Mom gave me one of the pills, after only a few minutes my body felt strange, actually euphoric. I'd never felt anything like that before, and it came in waves. The agonizing pain that I'd been in for hours was suddenly gone, and so was the mental pain I'd been suffering since being molested. It felt damn good. Little did I know the price I would pay for the rest of my life.

My childhood experiences were a taste of the prices and pitfalls of life. They were the first steps to my awakening, a continuous striving to learn as much as I could about how to make it BIG. And I continued to pay my own vig on every step of the journey.

# CHAPTER 2

## Teen Years and Becoming an Adult

**Teens, School, and Drugs**

Thanks to my injury, the summer of 1980 was pretty much a bust between surgery, doctor's appointments, crutches, and rehabilitation. Thankfully, I was off the crutches by the time I started high school. Even though I still hated school, one good thing did come out of that year: I became friends with kids I previously hated.

Competition in Little League was fierce, and we developed an immature hatred of opposing teams. At my homeroom "meet and greet" on the first day of school, I met some of my former rivals. We joked around and got to know each other in short order. We all seemed to have two things in common: wandering the streets and partying.

A lot of kids hung out in the small park in front of the school between classes to smoke weed and cigarettes, do whatever their drug of choice was, or just loiter. We mostly gathered in the middle of the park where there was a raised concrete circle painted to look like a Quaalude, a favorite of the students who did drugs.

I usually showed up to school carrying a newspaper and wearing inside-out sweatpants, a Bob Marley T-shirt, and moccasins. I knew I wasn't going to college, so my only interest in school was hanging out, period. But I loved to read and often cut classes and found my way to the library across the street. I spent a lot of time reading about things that interested me and avoiding anything related to the high school curriculum. I loved ancient civilizations and cultures, business, and biographies. My appetite for reading sometimes got me into trouble because I'd create my own five-finger discount and walk out with books I wanted to read. Even though they were free, I found a weird kind of value in stealing them.

One of the first kids I befriended that year was Joey. He was a baseball player from the next town over, and I'd played against his team during town games. He was the epitome of cool. With his street attitude, he walked around school wearing shades, jeans, and a leather jacket. To top it off, he always had a car, even when he was a freakin' freshman. We didn't ask too many questions because we were happy we had wheels. Whenever he came to my house, he parked his car down the street, so the adults wouldn't know he was driving.

One night he came to pick me up. Walking back to his car, he realized he'd left the car keys at my house. When we went back to get them, my father was standing on the front porch holding the keys. He handed them to Joey, and walked back into the house, shaking his head and muttering, "Fucking idiots."

Our adventures often took us across the George Washington Bridge during lunch to find some weed. The little tiendas lining the streets in Spanish Harlem had small pass-through slots in the front door. We'd slide five or ten bucks through the pass-through and out popped a nickel or dime bag of weed. All in all, it was a fifty-minute round trip with ten minutes to spare until class started.

The stores we could buy from changed unpredictably, usually because they got busted. When they were raided, it wasn't by the Mayberry police we were used to in Cliffside. These guys busted hard, closing down streets and coming in with tactical teams. We always hoped we'd never be around when a bust hit. But honestly, with all of us white boys crammed into Joey's car, we stuck out like a sore thumb. We were little degenerates who didn't know any better and didn't even care about knowing better. Like most teenagers, we thought we were invincible.

My high school years weren't just about skipping class and getting high. I found some healthier activities, like playing town league baseball. Mr. Sharp was my coach and one of my mentors. He called me his adopted son, the half-guinea Polack, and taught me to overcome my fears and win regardless of circumstances. Everyone wanted to play on his team because we got some pretty awesome perks and incentives. We traveled in either a Rolls Royce or limousine to away games, and Mr. Sharp ran our team like a business. He paid us $20 for each home run and $10 for each double play. If we won the game, we ate for free at one of his restaurants. But if we lost, we had to run the bases. Lots of bases. By this time, I weighed 180 pounds and swung an extremely heavy bat, so I earned lots of extra money and was able to party a lot during baseball season.

Mr. Sharp taught us to work together, but also to accept responsibility for our actions. He told us what we needed to hear, not what we wanted to hear, and I respected him for that. Mr. Sharp's antics definitely made for a unique baseball experience and being on his team expanded my experiences in a lot more ways than just learning to play better.

* * *

**Family Time and Getting Pinned**
My dad was an only child and had few cousins, so I was more exposed to my mom's strong Sicilian family. My mom's uncles were salty World War II veterans who eventually settled into lives owning stores and bars, and usually running numbers. They were average hard-working types and free-spirited characters.

My Uncle Vinnie was the rock star of the family, a larger-than-life figure in my upbringing. We never got along because we were too much alike. But I have to admit, he was one of my childhood idols. There was nobody, and I mean nobody, who messed with him. Ever.

We lived on a dead-end block, and he didn't care where he parked his car. It could be on the sidewalk or in a neighbor's driveway. Our neighbor next door was terrified of him, and Uncle Vinnie messed with him every chance he got. He often parked on the sidewalk blocking this neighbor's driveway, and the guy would knock on the door to ask politely when my uncle thought he might be leaving. We often laughed about this, because it had become a routine.

One time one of our cousins bought a used car, and it ended up being a lemon. When he went back to the lot, the salesman told him it was his problem...he was the one who bought it. Our cousin called Uncle Vinnie, and after Vinnie was done "talking" to the salesman, my cousin got to choose another car. That's just how he rolled.

Vinnie was very matter-of-fact about stuff. He hustled cars, trucks, and just about anything else he could fix, and he really put his passion into it. We'd ask him about a car he'd just fixed and he'd talk about how "I love that thing." Then somebody would come along and offer him $500 more than he thought it was worth, and he'd sell it to them. He was like that about everything: find something that needed fixing, fix it himself, and then sell it. I truly believe he was my inspiration for flipping houses later in life. I loved my end products, but if someone offered good currency, I'd sell it in a heartbeat.

On the other end of the family spectrum was my godfather, Uncle Adam, who lived with his partner, Charles, in Freeport, Long Island. "The Birdcage" could have been filmed at their house, there were always so many lively and flamboyant characters visiting. They had two Great Danes and one little ankle biter. When we pulled into the driveway for a visit, we'd hear the yapping of the little one and see the Danes or hear the low "woof" of the Danes and see the ankle biter. Being openly gay was generally not acceptable in those days, but in our family, nobody cared. Adam and Charles were beauticians and beautiful guys, and I loved them a lot.

There was a canal behind their house, and they had a beautiful six-passenger fishing boat. During the summers, I traded running in alleyways and hopping fences for fishing with my family and cousins. One of the upper-management guys from an artificial sweetener company lived next door, and he had a big boat with the company's name on it. The adults all laughed when they saw it, and my uncles wondered, "How the hell do you have a substitute for sugar?" Swimming off my uncle's boat in the Long Island Sound, we had the "Jaws" theme in our heads, thinking that the big sugar boat would be perfect. We all laughed at the fugazi artificial sugar executive, but I'm sure he's laughing now with so many food products being made from that crap.

There was an old-school icebox refrigerator in the garage where we kept drinks. It was never plugged in, we just used it like a cooler, keeping bags of ice in it with the drinks. It was in the early '80s on one of those beautiful early summer days, and we were all enjoying ourselves at the dock—music pumping, all the cousins fishing, boating, or swimming. I was hot and decided to get a drink from the icebox.

But that day, someone had plugged it in, not realizing it didn't work. Dripping wet, I grabbed the handle, felt a "zap," and screamed. My dad and Uncle Adam knew exactly what was happening and sprinted the fifty feet from the dock. They couldn't touch me, or they'd be electrocuted too, but someone pulled the plug and I flew back into the wall. I was dazed, and everyone gathered around to make sure I was okay.

Back then, if there was no blood and you were conscious, you didn't go to the hospital. I heard someone say, "Ask the kid if he wants a sausage sandwich." That was considered a cure-all with our crowd. After that incident, I seemed to hit a lot more home runs, so the family joked that it was because of the electrocution. It just may be so.

It didn't usually take such an extreme event to build my personal strength during those days. Sometimes those lessons came from facing my fears and testing my strength against someone else's, usually in a sports competition.

I used to go to professional wrestling matches with my family. I knew the matches were staged, but the wrestlers' skill and sheer strength made me want to wrestle. So in my sophomore year, I took up wrestling. The problem was that I sucked at it.

I had to trim down to qualify for the only weight class that was open. I was extremely competitive and did whatever I could think of to trim down, including taking Ex-Lax and cutting the inside of my gums so it hurt to eat.

Some of us went to the racquetball club and used the steam rooms, and when I went, I wore a rubber suit to intensify the effects. The old guys in the steam rooms thought I was insane and told me I'd deplete all the salt in my body. But being a brass-balled little shit, I just showed them the salt pills I took. They shook their heads because, really, how can anyone talk rationally to a kid who knows everything?

Our wrestling room wasn't very big, and there were two huge heaters that helped in the weight loss department. It got so hot that we tried to suck fresh air through the door cracks. Our coaches were the best at teaching us to overcome fear and pain, and they pushed us to the point of exhaustion, sometimes past our breaking points.

Before we even started practice, we ran from our high school to the George Washington Bridge and back. The extreme athletes-in-training ran across the bridge and then had to dodge bullets in Harlem as they ran. The physical training was brutal, and I loved it. If it hurt too much, I took a pain pill.

I lost my matches because I was constantly protecting my knee and not concentrating on what I needed to do. After the whistle, I was supposed to face off and wait for an opportunity to distract my opponent with a tap under the chin. But instead, I'd be waiting for an opening for a leg pull, and BAM, I was down and fighting my way back up. Each match was yet another loss. My coaches encouraged me the best they could, but I had my excuse ready: I'm weak from cutting weight and a bad knee, so there's nothing I can do.

One day we went to a match outside our district. I was nervous because I heard my opponent was a fucking monster. The whole way there, my coach asked me if I had a will prepared and if I was going to take the beating like a man. Talk about a mind fuck.

When we got there, one guy stood out. He was huge and muscular with a five o'clock shadow. He looked like someone's uncle, not some high school kid. My coach came up to me and said, "That's the guy who's going to put you out of your misery today." I stared and I was scared, wondering if I might actually need a will.

As the matches leading up to mine seemed to fly by, my coach sat me down and asked if I wanted to beat this guy. I said,

"Sure. Can I use a bat?" He took me by my face and said, "Pay attention, numb nuts. The only way you have a chance is if you distract him after the whistle. Come in like you're going for his legs and tap him under the chin. You'll have a split second to distract him, then go under him, put him in a fireman's carry, and pin him. That's your only option. Otherwise, he's going to put a hurting on you and mop the mat with your face."

I thought about it for a second, then couldn't remember if my coach said "wrestle" or "wait for a whistle to start the match." All I heard was the pounding heartbeat in my ears, and all I saw was my monster opponent breathing as he approached me. He moved side to side with his head moving up and down like a lumbering bull as he came into the center of the mat. But I took a deep breath and looked him straight in the eyes. Everything seemed to be playing in slow motion.

After the whistle, his head continued to bob as we came toward each other. On the downturn, I tapped him under the chin, causing the split-second reaction I needed. I went down on my knees, placed my right shoulder into his crotch, and lifted him off the floor. Once I got him in the fireman's carry, I turned to my left and pinned him. The whole place went silent, then suddenly the applause and cheering were deafening.

I'd won my first match. More importantly, I learned about the human mind, overcoming my fears, and psyching out both myself and my opponent. The thing is, this match was out-of-district so there wasn't any kind of scoring. It was merely practice. What I learned from that many years later is that all we do is practice for a show that's never real. I never wrestled again.

\*\*\*

## School and Work

In my junior year, I entered a work program for kids who wouldn't be going to college. Along with the work program, I took the minimum required classes and nothing more. I was in school at 8:30 and out by midday.

My first job was at a cartoon booth company that leased the booths to department stores in New Jersey and New York, and people paid a quarter to see a short cartoon. I signed for booths that came in for repair and checked the films to be sure they didn't skip. If a film skipped, I spliced and taped it, and then reviewed it to make sure it played smoothly.

There was a bonus to this job. When the booths came in for repair, nobody checked if the coin containers were empty. If there were quarters in there, I got to keep them. My boss didn't care because he was making money on the leases and he wasn't in the shop all that much. Also, when my friends came around, we partied and watched cartoons. Double bonus.

But the easy ride didn't last long. My boss' wife and kids came to the shop occasionally. They seemed nice enough. One day after I left work, I realized I'd forgotten something and went back to get it. I walked into the back office and saw my boss and his secretary in a very compromising position. I was fired the next day.

The fact was that, with or without a job, and whether I cut classes or not, I still had to go to school. My friends and I smoked weed or did hits of mescaline before class to make it more tolerable. I loved creative writing but often got into trouble in English class. My teacher encouraged us to push boundaries with our writing, being creative and detailed and vivid, but not as far as I often pushed them. She was very strict about homework and disciplined us when we didn't complete an assignment. I sucked at homework and was always handing it in late, but often managed to charm my way out of trouble.

Sometimes we had assignments with a writing partner. My writing partner, Antonio, was a beautiful kid in spirit—frail-looking, yet spunky. He carried his books with his arms crossed in front of his chest through the hallways. He was funny, with a geeky sense of humor that was very dry and highly intelligent. Although we hung out with different groups, I got to know him through class. We joked around and talked about Jimi Hendrix, Led Zeppelin, and the insane writings of our idol, Jim Morrison. We wrote like we were on hallucinogens, and most of the time we were. The words just flowed, and sometimes you needed an unbelievable imagination to follow our writing.

One time we had an assignment that had to be completed with our writing partner over the weekend. This was one of those times when we silently agreed we weren't going to do it, or that he'd just do it and let me share the credit, so I didn't talk to him that weekend. When I got to school on Monday morning and heard the tragic news, I was in a disbelieving shock along with a lot of the other kids. I really thought someone had made a huge mistake, but it was all over the school's PA system. First, we heard that Antonio was shot while buying drugs, but we didn't really believe that. By second period, the story was his best buddy killed him in a hunting accident.

That day, my English teacher was furious with me for not handing in my homework. She read me the riot act, asked me why it wasn't done, and said she would no longer accept my excuses. For some reason, she hadn't heard about Antonio's death. I asked her if she saw my writing partner in class that day, and she said no. I told her Antonio was killed over the weekend, and she never bothered me about my homework again.

I didn't hate all my classes. Our science teacher was one of the most popular in school and taking his class on mescaline was a trip. He was such a nice guy and had a reputation for being fair. He knew how to teach kids, and we learned more about life in his class than science.

Near the end of the year, there was a surprise in store for me. I was failing so badly, I would have to repeat my senior year, except my science teacher cut me a deal. I had to buy him five roast beef sandwiches and slither across the floor on my stomach while everyone chanted "LOSER." It was funny in a bizarre kind of way, and we all celebrated that I achieved the second-lowest grade in the history of his class. The honor of the lowest belonged to my brother, and my family was proud that I beat him. I did, however, make up much of the work, so I eventually passed—just barely.

The most interesting class I ever took was Mr. Norton's Business Law. He was very cool, sporting funky outfits and high-heeled boots, and he only started class after a Dunkin' Donuts run. If Mr. Phillips planted the seed, then Mr. Norton nurtured the seedling. He taught with stories and came up with tales that made us think. His class was the only one I ever thrived in because I loved the subject and his style of teaching. He wasn't teaching kids, he was preparing us to be young adults by using real-world examples. I'll never forget this man because he opened my eyes to the business world and made me want to work hard and own my own enterprises.

One thing I learned from him is that the "A" students teach the "B" students how to be employees to the "C" students. The A students are the ones who go to college to study how to be managers. The B students are the workforce who get trained to follow directions. The C students are the entrepreneurs who create businesses and tap into the already-trained workforce. This valuable mindset has stuck with me all my life as I applied that concept to serving my fellow humans in almost everything I do now. I can't sing this man's praises enough.

During my junior and senior years, I got one of my first real jobs. A friend's dad had a print shop right across the street from our school. I went to meet Louie, a short, stocky, gruff, crazy Sicilian guy with bags under his eyes. We talked about my family and the work that I'd done, and by the end of the interview, I had the position. He warned me that if I fooled around, he'd throw me out on my ass.

There were a lot of interesting characters working at the print shop. I shared jokes and our daily lottery picks with an older lady who'd been working there for decades and actually lived down the street from my house. The guy who worked the big presses was in his 70s and chain smoked. The two guys who worked the small press and collated were part-time firemen. Admin downstairs included a secretary, a father/son writing team, and a host of part-timers. We called the guy who did all the film development and photographic plates the Mole because he never left his darkroom. I met writers, photographers, mayors, politicians, businessmen and businesswomen, and a lot of society's more prestigious people.

My job started out pretty easy: empty trash bins, stock paper, sweep, and take care of the front parking lot. As Louie's trust in me grew, he gave me more responsibilities. I learned to melt and cast lead, which I did every few days. I took all the typeset from the big Heidelberg press down to the furnace, melted it all down, then poured the molten lead into the cast iron forms. I had to be sure the forms were completely dry, otherwise the lead bubbled, popped, and finally exploded. Sometimes I made ninja throwing stars and swords by pouring molten lead right onto the concrete floor and letting it cool. I never claimed to be bright.

I loved my job. At the end of each day, we all sat together smoking cigarettes and drinking coffee for about an hour, listening to the boss tell his great tales. He never admitted it, but I knew I'd grown on him when he started treating me like an adult. I made money while learning the trade, taking orders, using the collating machines, and ordering stock.

I constantly got into little screwups, but nothing serious. My boss had no qualms about calling me a fuckup, numb nuts, or shit-for-brains in his scruffy North Jersey accent. I once jokingly asked if there were any child labor laws about smelting lead. He pointed to the door and told me the only child labor law here was for me to get the fuck out. The best part of the job was I got out of school a couple hours before I needed to be at work. I wisely used that time to party with my friends in the city or go to the library.

One winter day, Louie was trying to get his car up the long, inclined ice-covered driveway. My buddy and I watched him slide from left to right, then right to left. He got out of the car and said, "You two better chop up that ice before someone gets killed." We complained about the generally shitty weather. He told us to stop bitching and start chipping, ending with, "I don't give a fuck how you do it. I don't care if you burn it. It better get cleaned."

We looked at each other and thought the same thing: Who wants to chip up this crap? We grabbed a can of gas from the garage, poured it on the icy snow, and lit it. We figured it would burn all the way down the forty-foot driveway. Amazed at our own genius, we watched the ice melt. But the water was now mixing with the gasoline, and somehow the flames traveled underneath the ice cover. Little patches of flame popped up in different areas. Full panic set in when one of these flames popped up under Louie's Cadillac. Just as I realized this wasn't such a good plan, Louie came blazing out the front door screaming, "My car blows up, you're both dead!" We responded with, "You said we could burn it." It took a lot of convincing for him not to fire me, and from that day on he called me Torch.

Along with all the good stuff, there's often something unexpected and bad. When I was seventeen, I heard that Larry, my friend from Little League, died from a drug overdose. I was devastated even though we'd grown apart and I only saw him occasionally. I swiped a bottle of vodka from our basement, sat in the parking lot where we used to play catch, got wasted, and cried for hours. I just could not think straight.

We hung out at his house more often than at mine because it was closer to the ball field, so I knew his family. Before he died, I sometimes bumped into his mom, and she always asked me to talk to him about getting cleaned up. I guess she didn't realize we didn't hang out the way we used to, and I had my own problems to deal with.

When I walked into the funeral parlor for the wake, my legs stopped moving. I was paralyzed by the idea of seeing him in his coffin. I finally got the nerve to walk up to the coffin, and I knelt on the kneeler in front of it. I closed my eyes and cursed him out and didn't stop until I felt arms wrap around me. For a moment, I thought he was hugging me. But when I opened my eyes, he was still lying in his coffin. His mom was trying to comfort me, even though she was crying hysterically. I lost all control, and just cried with her. I had to leave, and I didn't go to the funeral. I couldn't. I could not contain my emotions.

I realized then that my pills could help me blur out yet another emotional trauma. There was a lot of drug use going on in school, and I tried a lot of things to blot out what happened to me as a child. My mom started having complications from the car accident a few years before. Bills were piling up and frustration was high in my house, so I wanted to be anywhere but home. Now, another loss. And more drugs.

# CHAPTER 3

## Work, Florida, and Recovery

**Work and Business**

After high school, when I was about eighteen, my ambitions turned toward construction. I wanted more money than working part-time at the print shop would provide, so I quit and took a job for a fence company where I fell in love with carpentry. I installed wood fences and learned lots of tricks about the landscaping industry. I apprenticed for a few months, working day in and day out digging, mixing cement, cutting boards, and making custom wood fences. I was often left to problem solve any issues and found the job very interesting.

I quickly learned to do the job right the first time. The postholes had to be a minimum of two feet deep. Otherwise, when the ground defrosted in the spring, the fence posts shifted, and I had to repair the fence, often on my own dime. It was tough work because most of our jobs were in the Palisades where the ground is mostly bluestone. We had to use a gas-operated jackhammer to dig the postholes. It was a heavy sucker, and the vibrations wreaked havoc on my back and hands, but I loved the physicality.

A year into the job, my responsibilities grew. I was put in charge of ordering red cedar from Canada and metal pipe from Korea, and I got to know most of the gravel yards in Bergen and Hudson Counties. This is when my appetite for commodities kicked in. I quickly learned to order and store materials during the off-season when prices are lower, and then during the season, we could charge customers full price and pocket the difference.

I loved being treated like an adult and given lots of responsibilities, and I loved that I was making a lot of money. While my friends learned about widgets in college, I learned about life, responsibilities, and consequences. At nineteen, working full time plus some side jobs, I made more money than most of the adults at the fence company. One of my part-time jobs was delivering for one of Mr. Sharp's restaurants nights and weekends.

Growing up in a Sicilian family, I learned a lot about body language. I've been studying people's body language and "tells" since I was a kid playing baseball, and Mr. Norton, my high school business law teacher, taught me that using these skills would give me an edge in business and in interactions with people. Learning to read a person during a five-minute interaction was powerful to me, and I took that knowledge to the next level.

It can also be a curse because you know when someone is lying to your face. Being deceived by people you care about can be heart-wrenching. It may sound strange, but you can often predict events based on a person's tells. For example, when you tell a kid to go do something like a chore, you can pretty much tell by their physical response whether they're going to do it willingly, do it unwillingly and sloppily, or not do it at all no matter what they tell you verbally.

While working at Mr. Sharp's restaurant part-time, I learned about corporate structure and liability by watching how the owner and his partners set up and ran their businesses. I figured out that corporate liability layering is, literally, like making sandwiches. Layering the meats, cheeses, lettuce, tomatoes, and onions is like layering corporate structure. If you own a restaurant, you can be your own supplier and make money from both businesses. But if you make both businesses a corporation, you significantly reduce your liability. Most people can't tell the difference between a big corporation and a small one, so it's a different kind of deception. Learning all this stuff in my late teens was powerful.

When I was twenty, I'd earned enough to buy a brand-new, fully-loaded Chevy Cavalier complete with sunroof and sports package. Not only did I have a regular paycheck and money in my pocket, I discovered something that was new to me at the time – bank credit. It was the first time I took a loan for a major purchase, and I felt really good about the whole transaction. I was on my way to becoming a businessman who knew how to party. I was pompous, fearless, felt indestructible, and thought I knew it all.

✳ ✳ ✳

**Going to Florida**

My father tells the story about the night I came home, packed my clothes in a garbage bag, and told mom and him that I was going to Florida. A snowstorm was on its way to New Jersey, and I wanted to leave before it hit, so I kissed them both goodbye and was out the door. While Mom cried, Dad got up off the couch, locked the door behind me and said, "I guess he wanted to go to Florida." It became a long-standing joke in our family. For me, it started a habit of heading for Florida about every other winter.

My first experience in Florida was really cool. I drove all night and the next day to reach Port St. Lucie, about sixty miles north of West Palm Beach. Back then, it was really small, just a strip mall with a Publix, and miles away was a mall at Jensen Beach. I rented a house from some family friends and invited one of my buddies from back home to come on down.

I'd saved up enough money in Jersey that I didn't have to work for a while. For months, my routine was the same: wake up, go to the beach, play volleyball all day, and party all night. I left Jersey because I was partying way too much, so I guess it wasn't the best idea to move to South Florida during the height of the Miami drug wars. One night I got so fucked up, I woke up the next day on a banana barge in the Bahamas. That was the '80s for me: go to a club, party, and eventually either find my way home or end up crashing in an unfamiliar place.

After a while I got bored, so I took a part-time job as a bouncer at a marina club in Jensen Beach. It was a dream job: party all night, make sure shit didn't get out of hand, and throw any offending parties out on their asses.

One night, a guy pulled a beautiful yacht into the marina. A half hour later, another guy pulled up in a Porsche and chatted with the boat guy in the bar. Then the boat guy took off in the Porsche, and the Porsche guy sailed off in the yacht. Later, some cop friends told me it was probably a drug deal. Drugs on the yacht and cash in the car, a simple exchange, and they were on their way.

During my first winter in Florida, some of the people who played volleyball regularly decided to have a Christmas Eve service on the beach. None of us were particularly religious, but one of the women was a reverend. It was very simple, relaxed and pleasant, so peaceful with all the candles and everyone just hanging out. None of us could have imagined at the time the disaster that would strike the next month.

On January 28th, my neighbor, Massi, called to remind me about the launch of the space shuttle Challenger that day. I was excited because I'd never seen a launch, and I had a perfect view just outside my front door. A friend from Jersey was visiting, and he'd never seen one either, so we celebrated the launch and his new BMW with drinks. We watched the interviews with the astronauts on TV and then the countdown. With ten seconds left on the countdown, we went out to the street to watch the launch. The shuttle went up, and then the rockets went off in two directions from the billowing cloud. Not knowing that wasn't normal, my buddy and I just looked at each other and said, "Cool."

Just then, Massi called me from work. She frantically told me the shuttle had blown up and everyone on board was dead. I thought she was joking because I didn't have any previous experience to compare this launch to. I couldn't believe I had just witnessed history and one of the biggest tragedies of that time.

    The next month, my buddy had to get back to his landscaping company, and I decided it was time to get my ass back to work, too. The only natural thing to do was to race back to Jersey. Literally. Him in his BMW and me in my Chevy. I think it took about fifteen hours of zipping through traffic, a straight shot all the way there.

*  *  *

## Working in Jersey

By the midsummer of 1986, I was back to working for my buddy's landscape company until I blew out my knee again playing soccer. Over the next six months, I had two surgeries, lots of doctors' visits, butt loads of opiates, and plenty of physical therapy. I couldn't do physical work during all of this, so I needed to create a new income stream. A buddy of mine suggested we start laying odds on some games. I didn't have a clue how to do this, but I soon learned how to book. I rented a basement apartment from a Greek friend of mine, and we set up shop. What an endeavor that was—telephones ringing all day, watching games nights and weekends, and dealing with one degenerate gambler after another.

    I was naïve going in, and it didn't last very long because I didn't have the stomach for it. Want a teaser or parlay or chase-a-coin toss? We did it. If you let them, people would bet on two cockroaches crawling up a wall. Watching people throw their lives away on gambling never made sense to me. That being said, I'd rather be the guy laying the odds than the guy paying cash out of my pocket. But when you're booking, there are too many things to worry about: who's going to rat you out, who wants their cut, all the excuses why somebody can't pay you, and then when they do pay, they act like they're doing you a fucking favor.

This is where I learned about the vig, which would become a metaphor for my life. Every time I turned around, I was paying a vig for something. I realized the vig is something you never get back. Whether you win or lose, you have to pay something to the house. I eventually figured out that I wanted to be the house.

I felt better and could go back to work, so my Greek friend got me a welding job with his brother in Hoboken, and I learned some new skills, including burning steel. I knew some basic techniques from working at the fence company, but nothing too complicated. At this new job, we made fire escapes and worked a huge job at a pencil factory in New Jersey. At that point, I was willing to learn anything to make money.

Hoboken back in the 80s was mostly derelict buildings scattered throughout the city. There was talk of the town becoming a major player in the housing market, but I couldn't see that happening. Jobs were scarce, and nobody had cash except for the Greek and Italian masons I knew and worked with. They barely spoke English and had no formal education, but I watched these artisans slowly take over the city. They bought dilapidated houses for cash and then worked on them, fixing the foundations and putting in new columns and I-beam supports. I know this firsthand because I dug hundreds of column footings in their basements.

I was mentored by the guys I worked for, learning masonry, and framing houses and roofs. It was labor-intensive work, mixing concrete in buckets and climbing the side of a four-story scaffold, only to be yelled at for bringing the wrong consistency of mortar.

I was young and eager to learn from them. They bought a dilapidated multi-unit brownstone under a corporation separate from their construction business, and just sat on it. I learned what they did and how they did it, but I never paid attention to the "why." I didn't understand their mindset: buy a building for thousands, sacrifice now, hold on to it for twenty years, and sell it for millions. Which is exactly what they did.

Between the knee operations and the Jersey winters, I needed to change something and start making more money. Bills were piling up, I didn't have insurance, and I started getting threatening letters from the IRS. It was a mess. I was getting antsy, so decided to start my own construction company.

I subcontracted for some of the builders, and along with that came some heavy responsibilities. There was liability insurance, workers' comp, and all the other expenses involved in running a company. It got to the point where I was working just to pay my bills, and I began to realize that the more you make, the more you pay. You can work hard and succeed or work just as hard and fail because that's the crazy system we have.

These were not fun times for me. My mom was getting sicker from the effects of the car accident, and my parents started thinking about moving to Florida. I tried to help, taking her to doctors' appointments and giving what I could. Even though they had insurance, the bills were insane. It was hard watching them get beaten by the system. You can work your whole life and the system can still beat you down until you can't do anything else but walk away. And that's what they did. Somebody offered them an unbelievably high price on their house, so they packed up and moved to Florida.

* * *

**Drugs and Recovery**
When you're a drug addict, you have a sick secret. Nothing matters but the drugs. Absolutely nothing. Not relationships, business, school, family, morals, or personal ethics. It's all about finding your next high, even if you have to lie, cheat, steal, manipulate, connive, or in some cases, murder. You're depressed and mentally hurting from whatever trauma you've been through, whether it's physical, sexual, or mental, and only the drugs give you relief, even if it's just temporary.

It's often said drug addicts are helpless to their addiction, but I don't agree. I think we're afraid to look at ourselves in the mirror and face our pain naturally. Everybody hurts, and everybody is going through something every day. Yet some choose drugs to deal with it and become dependent on them. And we're mostly judgmental hypocrites when we point the finger at somebody for being addicted to illegal drugs when it's just as likely you can get addicted to legal substances like alcohol, tobacco, prescription medications, currency, politics, religion...take your pick.

After yet another knee operation and everything that entails, it all came crashing down. I was twenty-five and homeless, living on job sites in partially built structures I was working on. My construction company folded; I'd burned my bridges, and nobody trusted me. More people walked away from me then than at any other time in my life because I was doing way too many prescription pills, too much cocaine and Jack Daniels. It was a horrible time and, honestly, a life changer for me. Looking deep within, I found the person I was really hurting was myself. Then I chose to build a new life.

I eventually scraped up some money and found a little hole-in-the-wall basement apartment on Knox Avenue in Cliffside. That was my detox—all the shaking, throwing up, and sweating—with my asshole roommate smoking rock in the other room. I found support in Narcotics Anonymous, a quirky place where strangers tell each other all their personal problems, all trying to get better. But I changed my life in ninety days with ninety meetings. I started rebuilding by taking small jobs, handyman gigs, and working for a friend as a carpenter. I started walking for exercise, mostly to meetings.

During my rehab, I listened to stories about other people's fuck ups and addictions, stories more despicable than mine. I learned about the gang rapes, the physically tortuous relationships, and some of the worst of human suffering. I'd thought I was alone in my addiction and felt depressed and vulnerable. But now I was surrounded by doctors, lawyers, teachers, moms, dads, and even pastors, all with the same struggle. And I found out that no matter how bad I thought my life was, somebody always had it worse. I was creating a new foundation for my life, and things were really good for about a year. Then the bottom fell out again.

My knee gave out for the third time, and I needed yet another surgery. This time I was really scared because I didn't want to get trapped into taking prescription pills again. How the hell was I going to do this without pain medication? After the surgery, I did take some painkillers for the pain but gave the rest to a friend, so I wouldn't have them around.

Man, I was tired, and not a sleep-deprived kind of tired. My soul was tired. My NA sponsor gave me a cassette tape on self-hypnosis and a tape player, and my new addiction began. Now, instead of being a victim, I was hypnotizing myself into being victorious.

* * *

**Working, Learning, Driving**
With a new mindset, I began to realize I had the potential to be profitable despite the start of an economic collapse. About every other winter, I worked framing jobs in Florida, but that was no longer an option. Winter was fast approaching, and framing in New Jersey in the bitter cold was not something I wanted to do. Even after my company failed, I'd been able to get small remodeling jobs here and there, but those had also dried up. So I found a job driving a cab. Now I had another business to learn and I could hone my skills in understanding people, particularly through their body language.

The quickest way to learn about people is to get a job dealing with large numbers of individuals. I drove a cab from 6 pm to 6 am from the taxi stand near the George Washington Bridge in Fort Lee. I made decent money and was able to develop other skills at the same time. After I'd practically memorized the audio tape my sponsor had given me, the next one was on the mind and memory association. It taught me to put words into a story to better remember details. I bought just about every self-help program late night TV had to offer and became obsessed, listening to tapes all day and night.

All kinds of people rode in my cab, from executives and newscasters and celebrities, to everyday people. I struck up a conversation with all of them, all about harmless stuff, and watched their body language and facial tics in the rearview mirror. I guess you could say I was running my own social experiment.

It wasn't a good time to be a cab driver. The crack epidemic was in full force and people were desperate. Drivers were getting shot and robbed. We always tried to have a metal plate in the seat back of the driver's seat in case a rider tried to shoot us in the back. There were always spare car parts around the shop, and we got creative in making our makeshift body armor.

One night at about three o'clock in the morning, I picked up two guys in business suits who wanted to go to the Bronx. Something didn't feel right, but I headed there anyway.

Halfway across the George Washington Bridge, I heard the unmistakable sound of a shotgun being racked and a clip snapping into a handgun. I realized at that moment that I didn't have a metal plate in my seat back. I thought I was going to die. But the guys laughed, and one patted me on the shoulder and said, "Don't worry, it's not for you." I'm not gonna lie, I thought I needed to change my shorts after I dropped them off. I called it in to the dispatcher and flew back across the bridge.

My stint as a cab driver was definitely adventurous. I learned just about every street in Manhattan. The cab company was licensed in New Jersey, so we could drive fares into New York City, but couldn't pick up a new rider there. But if someone flagged us down, we all did it anyway.

Whenever we got pulled over, the cops checked the vehicle identification number and sometimes the VIN on the car didn't match the engine. I never expected the owner of the cab company was also running a chop shop, but he was. The cabs always looked great because as soon as a door, hood, rear end, or quarter panel came in, it was immediately painted. There was always some government agency investigating them, and eventually they got shut down.

Although it was a good gig, listening to tapes and meeting people, it was just too stressful not knowing if my car was legal or if I'd get shot, so I had to find something else. But even now, every time I get into a cab anywhere in the world, I wonder if the car is legal and the driver is safe.

This phase of my young adulthood added a lot of bizarre experiences to my life's resume, and each one left me even hungrier to learn about making money. Since I always wanted more, I never hesitated to jump in with both feet. I was always in search of the next opportunity. As it happened, the next opportunity took me to Paradise.

# CHAPTER 4

## Hawaii and Iniki

**Getting There and Settling In**

Life was a little upside down in Jersey in the early '90s. The construction industry was starting to take what would end up being a huge hit. Banks were calling in their loans, so buildings were being left unfinished all over Fort Lee, Cliffside Park, and Fairview. I was competing for kitchen and bathroom renovations against contractors whose high-rise building projects went belly-up. I didn't want to get stuck in another shitty real estate cycle. I needed some new money to pay off my debts and starting up another construction company didn't seem like an option. And I needed a break.

I saw an ad in *The Bergen Record* looking for carpenters to work in Hawaii. I called the guy, Pete, and after a little research—about ten minutes—I packed my bags. I didn't have a clue what it would be like and had no expectations. I just needed to make money and figured it had to be better than what I was facing in Jersey. My luggage consisted of some tools, my Jersey attitude, and a pair of brass balls.

The flight to Hawaii was long and there wasn't much to do besides drink, so I had a really good buzz brewing during the flight. Pete was supposed to pick me up at the airport and take me to the house where I'd be living. I waited for him for about an hour, but he never showed. I called him, but he didn't answer. I didn't know another goddamn person in Hawaii, so I called a cab. If there's one thing I know, it's the livery business. It's the same everywhere; for a small vig, and if the driver is good, you can learn a lot about a city in about thirty minutes.

I didn't realize Hawaiians spoke a different kind of English slang. I was having a conversation with my driver, but half the time I didn't really know what the guy was talking about. I was used to hearing other languages and dialects, but this one was completely new to me. This was definitely going to be another learning experience.

We drove around for a bit, and I saw how small Honolulu was. I had the driver take me to a rental agency so I could get a car, and I got a hotel room for the night.

When I finally stopped chasing my tail, I called my girlfriend back in Jersey and got some bad news. I'd seen her cousin the night before I left, and he died later that same night. This crazy-ass Jamaican thought his Toyota Corolla was a Porsche and crashed himself into a divider on the Cross Bronx Expressway.

This was a new kind of pain for me, and it was almost too hard to bear. I was 5,000 miles away from family and friends, and I couldn't just pick up and go during a crisis. Not being able to help was a new reality I would have to get used to. My first twenty-four hours in Hawaii really sucked, and the next few years proved difficult as well.

The next day, I went to the address Pete had given me, and he was there. He asked, "How'd you find this place?" and I replied, "Umm, a map." He had some houses and charged $500 rent per person. I got a room in a two-story house in Kaimuki. I found out later that Pete rented the house for $800 and charged each guy $500. Now that's not for a private bedroom, that's per person. Sometimes rooms had more than one occupant. Not bad cash if you have four five-bedroom houses.

After some informal introductions, I settled in. Everything was set up perfectly...or so I thought. When you've got five carpenters living together who all drink, smoke, get stoned, and are belligerent every day, life can be a little taxing. There was so much testosterone in that house, it was ridiculous. Mario the Italian and Otis the black guy were both from Brooklyn and went at it all the time.

That first day after a little pakalolo (Hawaiian for marijuana), we headed to Sandy Beach. To see how tough I was, Mario bet me I couldn't walk from the car to the water with no shoes. I thought, "Come on. Really?" So off I went, a none-too-bright Hawaii beach virgin. All I can say about that is, "holy shit," because the skin almost burned off the bottoms of my feet. I was digging in my bag for my flip flops, but Mario had taken them. Otis procured them, handed them to me, and said "Here, Bear. Maybe if we drown that wop's ass, we can all sleep better at night." Otis and I became instant friends.

As we all got to know each other, we fell into our respective places, hanging out and fighting each other almost nightly. Otis and I mostly hung out together while the others became drunken fools, pissing their money away and fighting the Hawaiians. Mario was the worst, calling the Hawaiians "saltwater niggers." Yeah, he didn't last long in Hawaii.

After settling in, next on the agenda was finding a job. The deal was Pete found carpenters on the mainland where work was scarce and imported them to Hawaii where there were jobs. He didn't set anyone up with jobs – we had to find them ourselves. He took me down to the union hall where, for $500, I got my union card and could immediately start working. Getting a union card in New York and New Jersey was nearly impossible if you didn't know the right person, but in a matter of hours I became a member of Hawaii Local 745.

I took the direct approach: I went to a construction site and talked to the foreman. In winter, I could always get a job in Waikiki because the locals were surfing all day. I mean, think about it. We lived in paradise. Why would anyone stress himself out trying to get rich? Our lives were already rich. May as well go surfing.

I went through a few jobs and ended up working on a pier near the USS Arizona Memorial. We framed knee walls and had to work on floating platforms to get to the part of the pier that needed work. Every time a boat went out to the Memorial, people dropped leis in the water, which floated past our platforms. The guys picked them up and took them home to their wives or girlfriends.

On that job, I walked on rebar for hours on end. Whether it was ninety-degree weather or pouring rain, we stayed and worked. The foreman was from Seattle, and in Seattle they don't stop working because of rain. I also learned how things really get built and how everything ties together. And I learned about regulations and cost overruns on government projects.

My friend, Nick, was an older guy in his late 50s. We met on a job and he took a liking to me because we talked about financial stuff. He was a huge influence on me because he taught me the difference between currency and money. He told me that making currency (cash) was easy, but making money was hard. To him, money was his friendships, his love of building things, and hanging out and working with the guys on the job sites.

He played the dollar markets in Asia and made thousands before most of us woke up for our morning coffee. He always laughed at me because I didn't understand why a guy making that kind of money played carpenter with a bunch of knuckleheads in the Hawaiian sun. He worked for the benefits and because he loved the camaraderie on the job site.

When we had lunch together, he told me that being happy with what he did in life made it feel like he wasn't really working. Nick definitely had a unique outlook and was always smiling. I was always happy to see him, and I'm glad our journeys crossed paths. I believe I have life beat because I always love what I'm doing at the time, and I learned that from Nick.

Within a couple of months, I began to like the culture. I learned about being a "haole" (a foreigner) and about being a "kama'iana" (someone who lives there). I was friendly with some

Hawaiians on the job sites, and before I knew it I was partying in Wai'anae and Waimānalo. In the early 90s, not many white boys got that privilege. Usually, one of two things happens within the first year of living on a 600-square-mile island. Either you get island fever and want to leave, or you love it. I experienced both.

I met a guy named Sato while playing volleyball at the park, and one day he invited me back to his house after a game. Some of my construction friends warned me that he was weird and said I was out of my mind to go. I didn't really know the guy, but never picked up a bad vibe from him. I knew he liked weed and hated drinking, so he sounded like a buddy to me.

Walking down the beach toward Sato's place, I passed several nice, big houses that needed renovation. I got to his old, ornate gate, which had a weird handle and bushes covering it up, so I figured Sato's house was one of those that needed renovation.

I came around a bend in the little winding path and noticed the landscaping was nicer and more professional than others in the neighborhood. From my experience landscaping in New Jersey, I could tell this must have cost hundreds of thousands of dollars. There were huge palms, circular paths, rock walls, and fountains made of granite and stacked stone. I came across a huge pool with several fountains in the middle and swimming lanes straddling the edges. On each side, there were tables with neatly covered umbrellas and seating for a couple dozen people.

There was a wide patio overlooking the pool and the pounding Pacific Ocean. It must have been a twenty-million-dollar view. There were housekeeping staff and groundskeepers all wearing aloha shirts and khaki pants. The place was gorgeous and worthy of any *Lifestyles of the Rich and Famous* episode.

I spotted Sato tending to a huge pile of cut marinated beef. He looked up at me and cocked his head like he was ready to explain something. He seemed to be waiting for the "shock and awe" most first-time visitors to the massive estate must have felt. I simply asked what he was making and what kind of marinade he was using. I saw relief in his face, followed by a huge smile. We started up our conversation where we had left off at the volleyball game.

Sato talked about Japanese culture and family, business, and the expectations of a family with old money. He sounded like someone spilling his guts, like he'd done something wrong because he was wealthy, and I just listened. He talked about entitlement and loneliness, never knowing if people liked him for himself or because of the money. The "lonely person" theme kept creeping back into the conversation; his parents traveled wherever they had business, mostly leaving him home alone.

The meat was amazing, sliced thin, Yakiniku style, served with calamari and bowls of steamed rice. Sato took out a bong, to the dismay of the staff, and we topped off our great meal with some hits while enjoying another beautiful Waikiki beach sunset. I looked around at this fabulous estate and the obvious wealth and found this kid with unbelievable resources was poorer than I could have imagined. He was graduating from college, and this "party" was kind of his graduation present. Here he was celebrating with someone he didn't know, with food and bong hits.

A few weeks later, he was on the cover of a Pacific Rim business journal, all smiles, with Dad passing the business down to Junior. I read their story at the Waikiki pier while surfers rode the waves and catamarans filled the surf for another amazing five-finger-of-God sunset. I was broke as hell, free to create or destroy whatever I wanted, and here he was with his life's path all laid out for him by his family. I wished him well.

※ ※ ※

## Doing Jobs and Shifting Gears

The job I had on Ford Island was one of the best. Man, it was unbelievable watching the groups of fighter planes flying into Hickam Air Force Base or squadrons of helicopters flying into Schofield. It was my first time on a government project, and quite honestly, my first exposure to the blatant overspending by the government. Years later, the project was featured in a magazine as one of the costliest overruns in history.

One day, a form blew out that held about five truckloads of cement. I couldn't believe it when we started tearing apart what took us weeks to prepare, and all that cement was just hosed into Pearl Harbor. While we were ripping the forms apart, someone passed me a two-by-four and a nail went through my hand. In through the palm and out the back. The medic quickly cleaned my hand and I went back to work. I didn't realize until later that as we were cleaning up the blowout, I was getting cement poisoning.

That night at home, my hand started to hurt like it was on fire. By early the next morning, it had swollen up and looked like a piece of raw meat. I couldn't bend my fingers or my wrist, so I went to the hospital. They gave me antibiotics for the infection and drugs for the pain. I was nervous about taking anything for the pain because of my past experience, but by the following morning, the swelling had reached my elbow. I checked into the hospital for observation. That evening, I had a high fever and the swelling had reached my shoulder.

The doctor warned me that I might lose my arm, and I told him I'd rather be dead. It was a pretty weird situation, thinking about being armless for the rest of my life, and I really started to lose it. At this point, my foreman was screaming at the surgeon that money wasn't an issue. The drugs were really starting to kick in, so I was semi-conscious when they prepped me for surgery. They would set drains first, and if that didn't work they'd take the arm off before the poison could kill me.

I kept my arm, and it only took a few months to heal. My recuperation was mostly learning how to use my hand again. But that injury has stayed with me. To this day, the muscles, tendons, and ligaments still hurt. Half the time my hand is numb, and carpal tunnel is a daily reality. It's just something I have to live with.

That injury changed the trajectory of what I imagined my life in Hawaii would be. Working union jobs was no longer possible, so I trained to be a businessman. I went to the beach in the morning, worked smaller carpentry jobs with Otis during the day, and drove a limo in Waikiki at night. I was really learning to hustle.

People were doing a lot of work on their houses and always needed good carpenters, so there were plenty of good side jobs. But materials were ridiculously expensive in Hawaii, from two-by-fours to nails. I priced my jobs based on the materials available on the island, but imported what I needed from the mainland, saving a bundle. I used connections from my construction days in Jersey and had contacts for cedar in Canada and Washington.

I had friends working at hotels and condos, and if something went wrong with a building, they called me first because I always made sure they got a little vig. It's just better business to help someone who's helped me.

Sometimes jobs didn't go as planned and I lost out. I worked on a guy's kitchen remodel on a time-and-material basis. He got a little behind on his end of the arrangement, so I was getting behind in my bills. When the job was done, I went to collect my final payment, but the guy died literally that day. It took a month to get my money, because, hey, how could I ask the family for money when their loved one just died? By then, I'd had to borrow more money to keep going, so once again my financial house was not in order.

I became a go-to guy driving limos for the ladies of the night because I made sure they made it to and from their appointments in one piece. Some were very smart and were in school for law or pre-med. I never judged them for their profession, I just figured it was another business. Most of the girls had fucked up family lives, and making cash using their bodies made sense for them. And where better to do that than one of the largest vacation spots in the world?

At that time, the average Japanese tourist family spent about $500 a day in paradise. At least that's what the wives thought. Often while mom and the kiddies slept at the hotel, daddy was off paying for a thousand-dollar-a-night call girl. I asked some of the girls if all that sex hurt and they told me about some of their tricks. Most of the johns were wealthy drunk businessmen or drunk military men on leave. It wasn't that hard to trick them, and who would the john complain to about getting ripped off by a prostitute?

I learned a lot about people from driving them around. Most of them were wasted and all they wanted to do was impress people and show off how much money they could burn. And talk...they loved to talk about this business or that business, and I was all ears. There were a lot of politicians from all over the world, so I heard some bizarre shit in the course of a ten- or twenty-minute ride.

On a really good night, I would get a call at five or six o'clock in the morning from a friend who worked at a hotel. They'd have a whale (someone with an ungodly amount of money) who wanted to take his family to the other end of the island. I drove them, then crashed on the beach for a few hours while the family hung out in some exotic cove or fantastic waterfall.

✳ ✳ ✳

## Iniki, the Strong and Piercing Wind

In the middle of the night, the warning sounded on the old World War II speakers that still hung from the tops of street poles. The ear-piercing alarm nearly knocked me out of bed. I had no idea what was going on, and I was scared. By morning, my roommates and I had gotten our bearings and realized it was going to be a long day.

At that time, Hurricane Iniki was the strongest storm to ever hit Hawaii. She sailed past the Hawaiian Islands to the south and hung out in the Pacific Ocean for a while. Then she turned to the northwest and then northward straight to Kauai as a Category 4 hurricane. I was living in a townhouse on the eastern side of Oahu, so didn't get the worst of it.

That day, I went to Eternity Beach and watched the waves crash up and over the highway. Yes, *over* the highway. The storm surge and tide smashed the rocks with incredible intensity. The wind was blowing so hard I saw a stop sign spinning, whirling around in its foundation. Yeah, I got out of the car to go see it, which in retrospect was really stupid.

When I got back to the house, the sea was rising up the steps of the little dock and back porch of our townhouse, one step at a time. Panic set in as I watched the water quickly rise until it reached the fifth step and I saw the neighborhood streets flooded by the sea. I'd never witnessed anything like it before.

I tried to call friends to find out what was happening in their neighborhoods, but phone service was sporadic at best. The radio was something of a comfort, reporting that our part of the island had been spared. But the western side didn't fare so well. I heard that the island of Kauai was a total and complete loss.

The single-wall construction of Hawaiian homes was no match for Iniki, and reconstruction started as soon as the storm passed and the waters receded. I wanted to head to Kauai to work but needed a sponsor of sorts. The scam artists from the mainland were already ripping off the locals, so only licensed contractors could work on the island. I got clearance through Pete, so I hopped on a local flight and witnessed the aftermath of my first totally destructive hurricane.

Watching the post-hurricane recovery and reconstruction left a bad taste in my mouth. Everybody in construction flew to Hawaii to get a piece of the settlement checks, just like ambulance chasers. Local contractors were letting mainlanders use their licenses for a cut of the profits.

New building codes had been put in place, and the newer codes made everything more expensive. Families got $100k from their insurance policy, and it ended up costing $200k to rebuild. The insurance companies made sure claims were processed and signed off fast so policyholders didn't have time to challenge the claim. The money was in the bank before the families could have a lawyer look at the claim. It was truly disgusting to watch this fraudulent system, but I got an education that would be put to the test in later years.

I didn't get a chance to work on the rebuilding on Kauai. By the time I got there, the locals were kicking the mainlanders out and taking over the reconstruction. There was no more work available, so I went back to Oahu and got back to hustling small jobs.

## Learning About Finance and Playing the Game

In between carpentry and livery jobs, I read the business section of the local papers. Business and real estate gurus were holding quick-start and long-weekend seminars, and people paid thousands of dollars to attend them. I could attend just about every seminar for $20 per day because in Hawaii there were always two prices: one for the locals and one for the tourists.

My world quickly got bigger, and my appetite for high finance and international business was now in full swing. I attended one seminar, and then another, and another, and before I knew it, I was knee deep with some of the best minds in the business world. I attended real estate classes and studied business law and international finance. No formal schooling, just lots of seminars.

I was quickly going broke and the bills were worse now than when I was in Jersey. I attended a seminar and learned I could get rid of my debt with the stroke of a judge's pen. I also learned one of the most valuable lessons of business: people will show you how to get out of debt, but you have to pay them first. What a concept—I had to borrow money to officially go broke. I was in my late twenties when I filed for bankruptcy protection.

I read a lot of Pacific Rim business journals and heard stories about international hustlers. A few of those stories really stuck with me. One was about a guy who purchased property on the east side of the island using one of his corporations who then sold it to another of his corporations. Corporation ABC sold the house to Corporation DEF for a million more than ABC paid for it. Then Corporation DEF sold it to Corporation GHI for another million more than DEF paid for it. With each sale, he passed the promissory note on the new money to another of his corporations. It was a trophy property with a lot of people interested in it, so each time he sold it, he put it in the paper.

Eventually, he caught a "whale" from Japan and sold that property for a few million more than the already jacked up price. Brilliant. He walked away a much richer man.

The flat-out cons were the funniest stories. During the Hawaiian real estate boom, a guy called a real estate company and told them he was coming to town. No big deal, right? Well, he used the name of a very famous Tokyo businessman, so the real estate company put him up at the best places in Waikiki and chauffeured him and his entourage to the best shows and restaurants, hoping he'd buy some property. Trophy properties in Diamond Head and on The Point cost millions, so spending thousands entertaining a whale was just good business. They only found out after he left that he'd conned them out of a really cool Hawaiian vacation. All he had to do was look at some houses in between sightseeing and scuba diving.

During this time, I attended a seminar by a real estate developer and professional speaker from the East Coast. I studied every move he made, from introductions, to backstage, to meet-and-greets.

During the afternoon session, the first thing he asked the audience was if we wanted to see a million dollars. Of course, everyone wanted to see it. What the hell were we there for, anyway? On stage, he pulled out a thick wallet and opened it. A credit card portfolio about twelve feet long flew out, and he said, "I never miss a business opportunity." He went on to explain about credit, credit lines, letters of intent, and other financial instruments that made my mouth water.

When he was done with that impressive feat, he asked if anyone in the audience was in bankruptcy. Never one to be shy,

I raised my hand. He brought me on stage, handed me a binder, and said, "Here's a free corporation." I was dumbfounded. I was in bankruptcy, I didn't have a product, and this guy just gave me a corporation. He explained that it was a Nevada Corporate Kit, and all I had to do was activate it. He would pay for everything as a gift for having the balls to raise my hand and fess up to being in a rather unfortunate financial situation. I thanked him and returned to my seat.

Then he explained that what I held in my hand was a new lease on life and a different way of looking at things. He further explained that in Nevada (at that time), you could be the President, Vice President, Secretary, and Treasurer of your corporation. As President, you could sell $50,000 in shares to you as Vice President. Then you, as Vice President, could sign a promissory note for the shares. Then you could go to a bank and get a loan based on the sale of the shares.

It felt like my head was going to spin right off my shoulders. How could this be? I thought I needed good credit to get credit. I didn't realize until then that corporate credit was an entirely different animal from personal credit. I was never taught any of this shit. A short time later, I found out that this is how the real world works.

I sunk every waking hour into learning about corporations. Legally, a corporation was a completely separate entity from the individual who formed it. You could get credit with an Employer Identification Number (EIN) instead of your personal social security number. I learned about corporate law and what corporations could and couldn't do.

If I became a corporation, I could go up against any other corporation, big or small, regardless of who was involved. The problem with being a guppy in the open water is that the sharks eat well using other people's money. The system is set up to keep the average Tom, Dick, and Harry out of the game. Figuring out how I could get currency was about learning how the system fails, then backtracking my way to success.

I attended a seminar about government real estate grants and loans, and particularly about urban renewal and how the government gives out money for revitalizing inner cities. I had read an article about Jersey City and Hudson County going through one of the largest renewals in history. Billions of dollars were being invested along the waterfront. When I was a kid, my father and uncles talked about the highway that would someday span from the George Washington Bridge down to Jersey City. It was a vision that materialized forty years later.

One day I was hanging out by the cliffs near Makapu'u Lookout thinking I needed to raise some quick cash. I only had a couple of grand left after the bankruptcy, and life's bills were catching up to me. So I took some money from my account and deposited a different amount the next day. The following day, I took out a different amount and then deposited another amount the next day. I did this every day for two banking cycles, then got a line of credit from the bank. All I did was use my own money to create a cash flow, and cash flow equaled credit. That's how banks worked at that time. It didn't matter how the money came in or how much of it went back out, they just wanted to see it come in.

This is the vig you pay yourself, scheming and manipulating your own shit. Some people don't have the stomach for it. But just because you don't know about something doesn't mean it's not being done to your bank account or pension plan. Somebody out there is manipulating it, and it's in the quadrillions in the derivative market.

* * *

**The Not-So-Great Side of Life**
I had a cargo van that I set up like a traveling shop. I arranged all my tools in the back, so it was easy to go from job to job. One day I had to park around the corner from my apartment. When I woke up the following morning, I walked around the corner and saw the vent window on the passenger side was wide open. All I could say was, "Oh shit." The van was picked clean. All my tools were gone and so was my briefcase, which I'd forgotten in the van.

The problem was made worse when I realized my checkbook was in the briefcase. It was a three-ring binder with three checks to a page and about fifty pages in total. I immediately went to the bank and closed the account. I thought that was the end of that until the local cops and the Feds came to my house every other day. Whoever stole the checkbook was writing checks all over Honolulu. What a friggin nightmare!

Most of my experiences with the locals were good except when I walked into the wrong place at the wrong time. My buddy from Brooklyn and I were driving to Wai'anae one day and stopped for coffee. I went into a very popular chain store that sells all the shittiest food and drinks in America. I got my coffee and added some creamer...you know, the free ones that are a single serving. Suddenly the cost of my coffee doubled. I asked what the hell was going on, and the owner said I had to pay for the creamers and that haoles shouldn't be in these parts.

I was really pissed off when I went outside and told my buddy what happened, but he just laughed at me. "Who said there's no such thing as racism in America?" He told me that one time he was running through a subway station and got stopped by cops. He was black, and he was running, and that can get you into trouble in some places. They asked him for identification, and when he opened his wallet the cops saw his credit card. They let him go because they said if someone has a credit card they probably won't commit a crime. He was as pissed off as I was at being treated differently because of our skin color.

Another incident made a much more profound impression on me. I was in 'Aiea in a strip mall behind the warehouse district and wanted to get something to eat. I was really craving a plate lunch, which is a standard Hawaiian meal of white rice, macaroni salad, and a meat entree. I went into a shop, and almost immediately my heart sank into my stomach. This little Japanese man went batshit crazy, screaming at me to get out. When I told some friends about it, they all laughed and told me that guy was known for throwing tantrums when hoales walked in.

I suppose I just wrote it off as cultural karma. I had a couple of friends whose families were rounded up and put in internment camps during World War II because of their

Japanese ancestry. They were Americans, mind you, sometimes fourth or fifth generation, and they were gathered up like animals. It didn't matter who they were, the contributions they'd made to society, or their value to their community. Their businesses and property were seized, and they lost everything. I can't even imagine the shit they had to go through. It made me even more cynical of the U.S. government.

After a few years of struggling against adversity, I decided it was time to throw in the beach towel and head back home. All my tools and shit I needed to make a living were gone, and again I found myself with no money or credit. The local economy was so insanely expensive that the average person couldn't make ends meet. It wasn't unusual to have three or four families living in a single-family house. My grandfather died while I was in Hawaii, and I had no way to get home for the funeral. Even the airlines' grief rate was beyond what I could afford, and booking a last-minute flight was impossible because they were always full. That was one of the experiences that tipped the scales toward returning home to Jersey.

I love the culture of Hawaii, all the good and all the bad. The Aloha Spirit will always live in my heart. The racism I encountered gave me a different perspective about white privilege, and it also gave me an edge. I witnessed and experienced firsthand how some groups are treated. I felt like I got a taste—just a taste—of hatred because of my skin color. In a bizarre way, I feel blessed to have had those experiences. I was able to see myself through other people's experiences and swore I would never look at people as a group with hatred in my heart.

# CHAPTER 5

## Back in Jersey

**Coming Home, Finding Work, and Dealing with Life**

When I came back to New Jersey with my tail between my legs, it was a humbling experience. But I was ready for another adventure. In Hawaii, I'd studied urban renewal and learned about government financing programs. So with my Hawaiian education and the Aloha I had found in my heart, I was confident and ready to hit the ground running. But first, I needed to hustle some work. I had no vehicle and no tools, but starting again from scratch was nothing new.

I figured I could do simple jobs like painting and masonry work without tools, so I made flyers advertising handyman services and passed them out in my neighborhood. Between jobs, I took a jitney bus to Jersey City to look at real estate, but that quickly got old. A trip that would have taken an hour or less with a car took most of the day. So I walked more streets, knocked on more doors, worked more jobs and, finally, one of my flyers landed on the desk of a dentist in Fort Lee. He happened to be my mom's dentist, and he'd known her for many years.

I took two buses to get to his office, which he wanted renovated. After negotiating the price and timing, I got the job. At last…a little bit of breathing room. The deposit was enough to buy a little four-speed mini pickup truck, and the job would pay for some basic tools. The truck was "special" because it came without a key. To start it, I had to jiggle the battery around and turn the ignition with a screwdriver.

Robbing Peter to pay Paul was the norm for me. I used the advances from new jobs to pay off old jobs. I had to keep five steps ahead of myself and always seemed to fall on my ass. Things are never the way you think they should be, and chaos was once again rearing its ugly head. I just kept putting one foot in front of the other. I was frustrated, though undaunted, rising professionally by buying houses through options, learning about mortgages, working handyman jobs, and trying to figure out how to get to Florida to see my mother before she passed away.

But at that point, I was acting like a victim, talking about my difficult circumstances instead of my blessings. I hadn't yet learned one of the most valuable lessons in life—how to respond to situations rather than reacting to them. In Hawaii, I'd met an old Japanese man at the polo fields who told me that in your twenties, make as many mistakes as you can; in your thirties, learn as much as you can; in your forties, make as much money as you can; so in your fifties, you've got life by the balls and can enjoy your mid-to-late years. I took it under advisement.

I was really missing Hawaii and one day found out a Japanese supermarket had opened in my old neighborhood. This was the beginning of the Asian invasion, the first of many Japanese businesses to grow there. I figured, what the hell, I'd practice my Japanese and grab some great food. As I walked into the place, there was a guy passing out flyers, so I went to get one. He looked at me and said, "Not for white people." It took everything I had not to slam this fucking guy into the wall. To say I was mad was an understatement. After the incidents in Hawaii, I swore I'd never look at people as different again, but that was naïve. I got so riled up, I looked up a lawyer in the phone book to find out what my rights were. This aggravating incident turned out to be a blessing in disguise.

I called a lawyer named Sean and met him at his office. He was a big Irish dude and was also very smart. Ultimately, there wasn't anything I could do about the exchange at the Japanese market because it was basically a "he said, he said" thing. I was pissed, and I wanted to change the world—another naïve notion. But it turned out to be one of those times when the student finally meets the teacher.

The Irishman and I became quick friends. We met for lunch and discussed business law. I was fascinated with corporations, what they could and couldn't do, the rules and regulations. I was tired of being a working donkey. I wanted something I could claim as mine—the American Dream—and I wanted it in contracts.

* * *

## Hustling Houses

I was tired of working as a contractor on other people's houses and getting screwed out of my last payment. People complain about contractors ripping them off, but there are plenty of property owners who know that if they keep the contractor coming back day after day for stupid little shit while they dangle that last payment in front of their face, the contractor eventually will stop coming back and give up on the money.

I needed to make some real money. I needed to have people calling me with offers on houses, instead of me tracking them down. With the real estate marketing tools I learned in Hawaii, I created some catchy ads and put them in a local Hudson County newspaper. It was pretty simple: "I'll buy your house or commercial property regardless of condition, with terms." As I'd hoped, the phone started ringing. I learned a lot about wild goose chases and wasting time and energy before I learned the most valuable lesson in real estate: prequalify the caller.

I was on a mission to provide affordable luxury housing in a blighted community—at least that was my intention. Jersey City had some beautiful vacant Victorian and brick row houses that needed to be rehabbed. Government grants and low-interest loans were plentiful. I put out some feelers to investors and approached some family members for opportunity capital. I thought something good would have to come out of it, but was I ever wrong.

I set up a corporation and began looking for houses close to public transportation. I focused on areas along the primary route, either at one of the planned Light Rail Transit stops or the secondary routes served by buses. My first run at redevelopment took me into an area where the blood was literally running in the streets, but it was a good place to start. If I could create a foundation in one of the worst neighborhoods, then the learning curve would be shorter. I considered myself a smart businessman but, in hindsight, I was mediocre at best.

If you want to get to know a neighborhood, drive around at two o'clock in the morning on weekends. You'll get a good feel for the area because at that time of night the neighborhood doesn't lie. What you see is what you get. You find out who's coming out of the bars, who hangs out on the corners, who drives by where, and when shots might ring out.

After I'd been at it for a while, I met with Sean more and more. I wanted to learn everything about real estate and contracts, and he was willing to teach me. I prided myself on being the guy with the info. I walked around with real estate contracts and promissory notes in my briefcase, ready to make a deal. I had my motivational tapes, tape player, a motivational book-of-the-week, a mortgage calculator, and lists of property owners looking to sell. I learned that the "deal of the century" usually happens about every other week.

I met a lot of people in Jersey City and got to know a lot of contractors, businessmen, money guys, and politicians. I canvassed streets and persuaded mailmen to look for houses in disrepair. I talked to contractors, paper boys, the public service guys, cops, and had at least ten real estate agents willing to send me leads. If I found a house I liked and came to terms with the owner, I did my usual 2:00 to 3:00 am neighborhood check, something I believe gave me an advantage over everybody else.

And whenever I cut a deal, I always paid a vig to the person who gave me the lead. How else would I get more leads?

※ ※ ※

**The Bergen Avenue House**
My brother and I went to look at a row house on Bergen Avenue. The day was hot, stereos blasted out of every passing car, kids sought relief from the heat with an open fire hydrant, and people went about their lives. But from the moment we arrived, we knew we were being watched by the entire neighborhood. They were probably wondering what the hell two white guys were doing there.

While we waited for the real estate broker, we checked out the exterior of the house and surrounding area. The building next door had long since been demolished, leaving an open lot and making this house seem like a corner property. A padlocked chain held the front door to its frame. The windows were all boarded up, but a peek through the cracks confirmed it needed a complete rehab.

The broker finally arrived and removed the lock and chain from the door. When we went inside, I took the chain and lock in with us. We'd heard stories of people going into an abandoned house and getting locked in. The building was then set on fire and the person inside burned along with the house. I didn't want to be trapped in an abandoned building for any reason.

Inside, the house smelled of mold, wet sheetrock, and garbage. Junkies broke in and used it as a shooting gallery. Just as we walked down the long hall, a huge rock came through the front door. I didn't blink, because I was on a mission, and it takes more than a rock to rattle my cage. My brother thought I'd completely lost my mind, but because of previous experiences, I was a lot more comfortable in that environment. I didn't buy the house, but that day has stuck with me all these years later.

* * *

**The Ocean Avenue House**
After looking at a couple dozen houses, I bought an old Victorian off the corner of Grand and Ocean Avenues. It was half a block from the park on a great bus route and within walking distance of a proposed Light Rail Transit station. If needed, it was a long, brisk walk to downtown Jersey City or Journal Square. As soon as I closed on the property, I dove in head first, setting up all the subcontractors, getting bids, filling out and filing government grant applications, and surviving a crash course in Hudson County street politics.

The myriad problems I would eventually face rattled me in ways I never thought possible. But it was another incredible journey, one I thought at times I wouldn't live through. The house didn't need a total rehab, just a retrofit. I didn't have to completely gut it, just cut the wood lathe and sheetrock up to two feet from the floor for the electrical wiring. But it quickly became the problem house—no problem too big or too small.

One day my construction crew wouldn't let me into the house. When I finally got in, I nearly cried. My electrician decided to rip out all the lathe and sheetrock on the walls and ceilings of the first floor and basement. Suddenly I wasn't in compliance with my original plans or my budget because the entire house now needed to be gutted. That added an extra $20,000 to an already tight budget.

The building inspectors began giving me shutdown notices. To make matters worse, I was seeing signs that I wouldn't be getting the grant money I'd been promised. I needed another five or so dumpsters to get rid of all the debris piling up in the front yard from gutting the three-story building. Panic and high blood pressure started to consume my life.

Every day, we had to sneak in the new electrical wire and copper piping, so it wouldn't be stolen before we installed it. I had a construction fence around the property and a few people watching it, but that only went so far. I walked in the door one morning to find $30,000 in copper and electrical wire ripped out of the walls, no doubt sold as scrap for a few hundred bucks. The crackheads were now plaguing the area, robbing all the rehabbed houses looking for anything they could steal and sell. I once saw two guys using three grocery carts to carry an aluminum light pole down the block. That's not something you see every day.

After losing my expensive materials, I decided it was time for some real security. I went to the Humane Society and found the most adorable twins. Thelma and Louise were sisters, an Akita/Rottweiler mix, and at about seven months old they were already seventy pounds. These girls and I were going to help each other out with our respective problems. I'd save them and give them a big home and food, and they'd protect the house from being robbed.

To keep people out, I ran a chain through the hole in the door where the knob used to be and around the doorjamb through a hole in the wall and secured it with a padlock. Over time, the dogs chewed on the hole in the wall, and eventually it was big enough for them to stick their heads out. It looked funny, walking by the house and seeing this massive dog head sticking out. People were frightened. It was good security.

I also got friendly with my neighbors. The house to the left was home to a very nice family of four, and an uncle and grandmother. On the right was a former teacher, now an unemployed crack addict. I became a fixture in the neighborhood and made friends. I went to neighborhood meetings, attended networking dinners, and learned the who's who in the political scene. I wasn't impressed with the thuggery but wrote it off as just part of the vig I had to pay to succeed.

By the time Thelma and Louise were about a year and a half old, they weighed one hundred twenty and ninety pounds respectively. They were the size of Akitas, but with Rottweiler markings. The neighborhood called them the devil dogs. I walked them at the end of a heavy link chain that split on a swivel, one side for each dog. People crossed the street just to avoid walking past us.

The girls ate a lot of restaurant scraps—brown stewed chicken, jerk chicken, oxtail, curry goat...you name it, they ate it. They ate neighborhood cats, the remains of which they left in the closets, the gutted rooms, and even the backyard. They had a huge house to roam around in and a decent-sized backyard, but Louise was smart enough to test the fence. When she found a weak spot, she either dug under it or climbed over it. Have you ever seen a dog walk up a ladder, or climb down one? It was like that. I got calls at all hours of the day and night from the grandma next door or the reverend down the street telling me she was out again. She wasn't vicious, she was just damn big and scary looking.

Even though the house was gutted and had no heat, bad weather didn't seem to bother them. One afternoon it started snowing, the first snow I'd seen since I returned from Hawaii. I didn't know it at the time, but a blizzard was coming in. I walked from downtown to the Ocean Avenue house to check on the girls in the middle of the snowstorm. I took some blankets and slept with the girls that night. They kept me warm.

What I learned from the Ocean Avenue house is that when you're an entrepreneur, everything goes wrong all the time, things come up that you simply couldn't have foreseen, and you have to be on your toes. Things can always get worse than you ever imagined, and you've got to solve problems quickly. It's a completely different mindset from a nine-to-five job and a paycheck at the end of the week. Eventually I was able to sell the property. But that's a story for another time.

✳ ✳ ✳

**Losing Mom and Running a Crazy Café**
All the fun and games didn't stop me from traveling to Florida to see my mom in hospice. The last time I visited her, she was heavily sedated and not very responsive. I was sitting by her bed holding her hand when she cried out, "No! No, Carol! No!" She kept repeating her pleas for a couple of minutes and then

calmed down. I left her room and asked my father who Carol was. He told me she was the Aunt Cookie who'd been institutionalized pretty much my whole life, but I'd never known her as Carol.

That night my dad got a call from the institution telling him Carol had passed away that afternoon. I think about it now and wonder if there's something more after this life. Maybe Carol was asking my mom to come with her, but it wasn't her time yet. Mom's time came two weeks later. I was back in Jersey City when I got the call that she passed away.

Some might take what I'm going to say next the wrong way. When I got that call, it was one of the happiest days of my life. She was no longer in pain, didn't have to go through any more surgeries, didn't have to take the drug cocktails concocted and tested on her like she was a guinea pig. She was finally free. Free from the TMJ that wreaked havoc on her life, the colostomy bag she had for years, and the joint replacements that never quite gave her the mobility she had hoped for.

It was also a sigh of relief for Dad and my brother and sister-in-law, who'd all been taking care of her. She was sick for over fifteen years, and now all the challenges of caring for someone with chronic illness were gone. My sister was devastated because she hadn't been able to do much from New Jersey. I was devastated. And I was tired. But I was finally able to cry. Cry at her wake, cry at the church, cry about my life. But I was happy I was doing it sober. It was the end of a long journey.

I was still dealing with ups and downs, still reacting to everything around me. I was an emotional mess, and the woman who showed me how to keep getting up every morning to conquer a new day was gone. But now I had an angel over my shoulder. That meant she could see everything I was doing. It was time to get my shit together.

Despite—or maybe because of—the house rehab deals I was working on, I needed to make more money. I found an opportunity to buy a small deli downtown. The owner needed to sell it, so I cut him a deal and took over. The only problem was there was already an Italian bakery down the street, two around the corner, and three more two blocks away. The neighborhood didn't need another Italian deli, so I turned it into a small Jamaican restaurant and named it after my mom—Lorraine's Café. A friend helped me cook in exchange for letting him prepare the food for his Jamaican café a couple of miles away. He didn't have a kitchen at his place, so he and his uncle used buffet trays and heat lamps to keep the food warm. We all did whatever we could to make things work.

It proved to be another time that I was way ahead of the curve. Everybody thought I was completely insane for opening the place, but it worked pretty well for a little while. I was attracting people from the neighboring city of Hoboken, and that felt good. But my neighbors were not thrilled with a Jamaican restaurant in the middle of their Italian neighborhood. Now, I'm talking diehard Italians here, the type who have no censors. I was taking a lot of shit from certain guys with comments like, "Hey kid, what do you expect...you got niggers in the kitchen," or "I know this place is a front for something."

The restaurant business always seemed great in the movies; the Italian's had Italian delis, the Poles had pierogis, and the Jewish guys had bagel shops. But this half-guinea Slovak had a Jamaican restaurant. It seemed logical to me at the time, and nobody ever questioned my balls.

* * *

**Newark Avenue House**
About a month after my mom's death, I got back into the swing of things. A friend had a building on Newark Avenue in downtown Jersey City that needed a complete rehab. It was huge; four 2,000-square-foot floors, ten-foot ceilings, and an exposed brick exterior. There was major roof damage, and the air inside was filled with the stench of pigeon shit mixed with mold and mildew from the waterlogged floors and ceilings. Two sections of the staircase were missing, and bricks periodically fell off the exterior façade.

    The building was a huge liability for my friend. He owned several houses in downtown and was enrolled in a program that went bust because of the federal government shutdown. It wouldn't cost me anything to take the option on the building, so that's what I did. I planned to sell it and invest the proceeds in the Ocean Avenue house, which was drowning in debt.

    It was a taxing time. I had to be at Ocean Avenue to take care of the dogs and keep the place secured from being robbed. I was working part-time at a mortgage company, so I could learn the business and needed to increase my hours on the floor. I was running the café, and I still had to pick up odd jobs to pay my bills. I stopped paying the mortgage, waiting to bundle it with other deals. But the person who held the note, the mother of a powerful local politician, was making noise, so city officials kept blocking my efforts on the rehab. I was going through all the right channels but kept coming up short. There wasn't enough time in the day. I was burned out, tired, and emotionally drained.

I finally got so fed up that I got radical. I found a half-sheet of plywood, wrote "For Sale by Owner" and my phone number on it in magic marker, and put it in front of the building. No fancy signs, no more ads in the paper, just a simple sign from a defeated man.

Sometime later I got a call from a guy with a heavy Indian accent. We set a time to view the building, and he came with his daughter. I was surprised to see a father and daughter team willing to take on a project this big. Although they didn't buy the building, I exchanged numbers with his daughter, Jane, and we kept in contact. I didn't know it at the time that, but I'd just run into one of those people who would be around for the rest of my life. We just clicked, talking and sharing ideas, and soon we became friends. She stopped by the restaurant and we went over contracts and talked about real estate and life. She's a very driven person, very motivated and tough on the exterior. But she's also one of those cool friends I could talk to about anything and everything, and honestly not have a care in the world.

One afternoon she called and said she wanted to meet up to say goodbye. She and her boyfriend came to my apartment and told me she was going to Africa for six months. I told her to send me a postcard and we'd get together when she got back. I wished her well.

The next call was from a guy named Ted. He bragged about what a great real estate businessman he was and wanted me to meet him at his office to discuss the building.

When I sat down with this fine gentleman, he condescendingly told me that when I got to his level, I wouldn't have to sell properties anymore—I could just maintain them like he did. I felt like reaching across the desk and slamming his head into it. What a pompous douche.

We agreed on a deal, and I met with Sean to go over it. Ted would pay me a transfer fee and pay off the mortgage and back taxes, all in one neat little package. Honestly, at that point in my life, I didn't give two shits what he did with the property. I just wanted out.

Before the closing, Ted called me back to his office and asked for my assessment of the property. I told him that bricks fell off the façade occasionally, something he knew from our first conversation, and an entire section needed to be replaced. He asked about the building's front façade and the windows, and I told him to just board them up for now. Repairing the brick façade was the priority. Sean and I went to Ted's attorney's office and we closed the deal.

A few weeks later, I drove by the building and was astonished to see he'd installed brand-new windows right over the top of the crumbling brick façade. I had to pull over because I was laughing so hard. A few days after that, Ted called and said he sold the building and he was going to clear $100,000. Again, he assured me that one day when I was successful, I could make that kind of money. I congratulated him and wished him well, even though I didn't feel it in my heart. He was so full of himself.

The day before his closing was scheduled, I drove by the property again. I was so astonished, I had to stop and get out of the car. The fucking building was gone. The entire building. Turned out that two days before the closing date, a brick fell off the façade and hit the windshield of a parked car, just as a fire marshal drove past. The building was demolished, and the sale never closed. He ended up eating the $100,000 and on top of that, the city charged him $20,000 to demolish it.

*** 

**Shitty Living Conditions and Shit That Happened**
I'd lived in about a dozen different places over the years, most of them not so great. Now I was living in a rowhouse apartment across the street from the Jersey City courthouse because I figured it would be an advantage when I needed to do research on real estate. In the mid-to-late 90s, downtown was not what it is today. It was dangerous. And I mean, you could go to the river and get robbed, mugged, raped—you name it, it could and would happen.

I was in this crappy little apartment and started having problems with my landlord. It was winter, and the heat didn't reach the top floor, so I had to sleep in my kitchen with the stove on. I'd done a huge weekend floor job and had enough peel-and-stick tile left over to cover the floor in my apartment. I just wanted a nicer place to lay my head, and it's amazing what a new floor can do for a place.

The no-heat thing was really causing problems, and I continued to freeze. Then the landlord told me I had to leave because the furnace was now dead, and he had to put in a whole new heating system. And I'd just put down all that new tile a few weeks earlier. So I uninstalled my floor. I sat over every single one of those tiles—900 square feet of them—with a hairdryer, melted the glue, peeled them up one at a time, and put them on wax paper. It took hours.

When the landlord came up and saw the apartment, the expression on his face was priceless. He thought he'd be walking on a new floor, but instead, with every step he took, his shoes stuck in the glue. It might sound harsh, but I had no sympathy for the guy. The money I'd been saving by living there was now all pissed away because I had to cut a deal with somebody else for another place to live.

I found another apartment on Brunswick Street on the north side by the ballfield and train tracks. I didn't have to pay a security deposit or first month's rent; in exchange for helping clean the place up, including hanging sheetrock on the ceiling. I was still able to walk all over downtown Jersey City and up to the dogs at the Ocean Avenue house if my truck ever broke down.

I walked a lot in those days, often just to clear my head. I often found myself down by the Colgate sign along the Hudson River where the city later built a park. Back then, it was just an empty lot with piles of garbage, and there was a huge concrete slab slanted into the river. It could fit five or six people laying down, and I could stare at the stars or at the beautiful view of the Statue of Liberty or World Trade Center across the river. Sometimes I brought Thelma and Louise, so they could run while I sat there and thought about life for hours.

One day after I'd taken the dogs for their walk, I headed back to my apartment. I could have taken the bus, but I wanted to walk. As I got to Communipaw Avenue and Grand Street, a kid came out of a store, got on his bicycle, and intentionally blocked my path on the sidewalk. In an instant, he took a gun out of his pocket, put it to my forehead and said, "I should kill you." Before I could react, a friend's cousin walked out of his store, smacked the kid upside the head, and hold him to put the gun back in his pocket. It all happened so fast, I was stunned.

When it was over and I was walking away, I chuckled to myself. All I could think was that he could've just put me out of my misery. At that point, I would have been glad.

One beautiful spring day, I was excited about the progress I was making on the Ocean Avenue house, a rare feeling for me in those days. I had to have the utility company install a new waterline, which required breaking up the sidewalk in front of the building. After weeks of waiting, they finally came and installed the new meters. Now I could pour the sidewalk and avoid a fine from the city or a lawsuit from pedestrians tripping over the hole. What a relief.

The cement truck arrived on time and everything went flawlessly. I put caution tape across the new sidewalk, attaching one end to my truck's mirror and the other to a bucket filled with cement. Nice and visible for all to see.

Later, I was looking out the window on the second floor when I noticed a man walking right through the tape. I yelled at him to stop, but he kept trudging through the new cement. He picked up my bucket of concrete by the handle, swung it hard, and shattered the window of my truck. Just as I got to the sidewalk, I saw Bucket Man punch a passerby in the throat. The guy was knocked out before he hit the ground.

I was about ten yards behind Bucket Man, and about thirty yards behind me was a crowd running after him. We'd all just crossed the street, and he walked toward a mother with a baby in a carriage and a little girl playing on the sidewalk. It all happened so fast. The man reached into the carriage, grabbed the baby like a football, and threw the child against a light pole. He turned to kick the little girl but slipped and fell before he could connect.

The air filled with screams as the crowd reached him, and it turned into complete mayhem. People grabbed garbage cans, sticks, rocks, fence gates, anything they could find to throw at the guy. Police came from side streets, parked on the sidewalks, and broke up the crowd. I could not believe the stomping this guy got from well over a couple hundred people.

I later found out this guy had simply walked out of the psych ward at the hospital about ten blocks away. He began his reign of terror in the hospital parking lot and continued from there, leaving a dozen victims in his wake. Just random people of all ages and races, men and women going about their daily business, never guessing when they left their homes that they'd come face to face with a creature of such profound evil.

I'd never seen the eyes of a madman before. Blackened, with no whites in his eyes. I have never witnessed such brutality as I did that day, and I hope I never will.

✳ ✳ ✳

**The Archangel and Getting the Hell Outta Jersey**

I started looking for the gentler side of life in everything I did and met an incredible human some people called the Archangel. This man was proficient in many martial arts, was a micro mosaic master, and knew everything about anything. When he played the guitar, tears would stream down your face. His name was Dante.

We quickly became friends, and I was interested in everything he had to say. He was Sicilian, about fifteen years older than me, born and raised in Jersey City. People used to say he was a savant, that his IQ was off the charts. I just found him interesting.

Our buddy Hanze had a store where we hung out, and he talked about his place in Jamaica: fifteen acres with a stream at the top of the property and a river running through the middle of it. The more we talked, the more interested Dante and I got in going to visit Jamaica. Hanze said we could use his property, so we decided to check it out.

I arranged for my responsibilities to be covered, flew to Jamaica, and stayed at Hanze's place for a week. It was a hut in the middle of the bush with no running water or electricity, but I could walk down to the sea. I instantly fell in love. At that time, I was ready to drop everything and go meditate on life. Back in Jersey City, Dante and I hatched a plan. We would move there with all my tools and build some cottages and tree houses on the property.

I decided to get rid of the restaurant and sold everything that wasn't nailed down. I'd leased the space but owned all the equipment. The landlord was pissed that I was selling all the stuff that made it a restaurant. It wasn't my fault this guy signed something he didn't understand, and his attorney said there was nothing he could do. He was so angry, he tried to hire a biker gang to tune me up. It didn't work because my friends knew the bikers and told them to back off.

Then he made threatening phone calls and whispered in the ear of anybody who would listen. One day he called and told me he'd hired somebody to kill me. I'll tell you, I was nervous. I kept looking over my shoulder until I had my bags packed and was on my way to Jamaica. The word on the street was that he had another biker gang looking to take care of me.

I found a buyer for the Ocean Avenue house who agreed to take the dogs and take care of the property until I came back to close the deal. It worked out really well. I saw Thelma and Louise one last time, gave them each a kiss, and said my goodbyes.

I packed up all my stuff at Hanze's store, labeling all the job boxes that would be shipped to Jamaica. A buddy told me to be careful because not everything they said about Jamaica was true. I didn't care; it was one more adventure, one I was really looking forward to.

The night before I left, I felt run down and was getting a high fever. Dante helped me with the last of the packing and finished it up so I could sleep. The next morning, I flew to Kingston.

# CHAPTER 6

## Jamaica, Mon

**The Plan and Life in Jamaica**

The plan was simple. I flew down to Jamaica, Hanze would ship my stuff to me, and Dante would follow a month or so later. For a long time, I'd wanted to create a special place for people to go to heal from their lives. We would build some simple cottages and tree houses and have people come stay for as long as they needed to.

My arrival was somewhat inauspicious. I was sick with a high fever when I left Jersey, took a shot of rum to knock myself out on the plane, and arrived in Kingston just as sick. I grabbed my bag off the airport carousel and walked out the double doors into pure chaos. The moment I stepped outside, my senses were bombarded, from the burning piles of wood and garbage wafting past my nose, to the cacophony of street hustle punishing my ears.

One of Hanze's friends had come down with me to stay at the hut for a while, and he'd arranged his own car. But he was scared shitless to drive in a foreign country. What a pussy, I thought, give me the fucking keys. Even though I was still sick, I drove. I was so tired, I just wanted to get to the hut as fast as possible.

Driving through the backcountry of Jamaica is perilous under the best of circumstances. The twists, quick ups and downs, and sharp turns make for a difficult journey. You can drive a few miles with no problems, then suddenly you're stuck in traffic watching a semitruck trying to navigate a hairpin turn while keeping clear of the hundred-foot drop off a cliff.

Adding to the natural perils of the terrain was the fact that I shouldn't have been driving at all. I ended up being "that guy" who caused everyone to be late to work or school or the market because I was driving while delirious and totaled the car. I barely escaped with my life. My terrified passenger and I were both lucky that day.

Once I got to the hut, I opened all with windows upstairs and laid down for some much-needed sleep, wearing just a pair of shorts. While I slept, it rained, and then the sun came out. Dreads and frequent visitors know what that means. I woke up swatting my hands around, looked down at my arms and legs, and jumped straight up off the floor. I was covered from head to toe in mosquitoes. There are multiple species in Jamaica. I was being devoured by what the locals call white caps, which feed during the day and leave bites like the ravages of a sadistic vampire. Lesson learned.

Despite my somewhat questionable beginning, I quickly settled into a lifestyle I'd previously only imagined was possible. The hut had two levels, each basically open space with sleeping bags on the floor. No electricity, no running water, no kitchen, and an outhouse with an amazing view. We just had to be sure to bring a stick with us when we went to do our business and whack the hole to scare away any critters before we sat down.

The road to get to the hut was called Pump House Road. There was a water station with a pump house that serviced the houses in the community, providing drinking, cooking, and bathing water. I sometimes saw chemicals by the pump house, so we didn't use that water except in emergencies. Our water came from a sweet, cold bubbling spring a nice walk from the hut. The walk took me past a beautiful waterfall where I ritually bathed myself. I sat back against the rocks and let gallons upon gallons of cool water cascade down on me, washing my thoughts downstream.

Dante came down about a month after I'd arrived, and we quickly settled into a uniquely agreeable and peaceful life. We smoked weed and ate unbelievably well, and he taught me martial arts and meditation. He helped me turn my mind into a sanctuary and enhance my senses. We walked the bush by moonlight, experiencing the wilds like the locals. I practiced blocking strikes with my eyes closed and swung a staff for hours as Dante played raaga on his guitar. Dante knew about art, music, rhythm, and tempo, and showed me how everything was connected. It's amazing how your senses change when you're pulled out of your normal "civilized" environment and dropped into one of calm and chaotic nature.

Most days consisted of the same peaceful routine. We at fruit with spring water in the morning followed by coffee and a spliff. Then some martial arts and meditation, either by the waterfall or by the sea. We went to the beach with our machetes and a staff and no water. When we got thirsty, we cut a long length of bamboo and whacked down coconuts to drink.

Not far away at Windsor Castle, there was a brackish pond about thirty feet from the sea. We often meditated there, with the stones lining the beach sending a harmony into the air as the water came in and receded. We walked to and from the pond, gathering the wood and debris washed downstream by flash floods and deposited by the sea. We made huge piles every couple hundred yards along the cove, some fifteen feet or higher. Nearly every full moon, we lit the piles, the moonlight enhanced by the raging bonfires lining the cove. Truly a beautiful experience, and a sight I'll cherish forever.

Most often the water was crystal clear and fresh, teeming with big blue crabs we caught and took home for dinner. We steamed the big claws and ate them with fresh vegetables. Thanks to my new lifestyle, weight was shedding from my body, to the relief of my distressed knees. In two months I lost thirty pounds. My goal was to get down to two hundred and ten pounds.

My solitude was walking. Not just "taking a walk" for a couple of miles, but walking from town to town, sometimes ten miles or more, with my pack on my back just admiring the beauty of Jamaica. But I always had to be aware on those tight roads because a car might come screaming past me. The vegetation was so thick on the side of the road that I could just lean into the weeds and they'd support the pack and me. But I had to time it just right, or the weeds would bounce my body right back into the road with the car speeding past. It was quite a rush, especially at night.

One of my favorite places to visit was Earth Mother's place. She was like a hobbit in the hills. I had to cross a river to get there, and I could only see her when it wasn't raining. She'd moved into her open A-frame house after her son died of poisoning. The walls were floor-to-ceiling shelves filled with jars full of teas and roots, and this was where I was turned on to natural solutions for health. It was an amazing place to meditate.

But it could be hazardous when I was caught there in a storm. When the clouds rolled in, I packed up and ran through the downpour and ended up sliding down the hill on my butt in a stream like an escalator to the riverbed. I hauled ass as the stream gradually turned into a river, an intense experience trying to beat the water down the hill to the road. It was a pain in the ass to try to get back up the hill since every path up was streaming down with water.

Three of the craziest and most revealing days I spent in Jamaica were spent in complete solitude in a circle, called the Circle of Life. I was told I could stay in the circle for three days, five days, or seven days. I chose three. I made my fifteen-foot circle on a piece of ground with a really good view within earshot of the river. I had enough fruits and vegetables for three days and plenty of coconuts. I had water and wood for a fire. The only time I left the circle was to relieve myself.

The first day was pleasant enough. I listened to the sounds of nature and examined every tree, nook, and cranny within eyeshot. As night came on, so did the bugs. I kept a fire going but still felt all kinds of things crawling on me. The mosquitoes were relentless.

As night turned to day, I heard the roosters waking and smelled the morning cooking fires nearby. My mind started to clear as I thought about my childhood, my teen years, and my young-adult life. I sat there and contemplated all my failures, my mom passing away, my bankruptcy, and all the stuff that went along with being an entrepreneur. It seemed like one failure, or "experience," after another, and I was tired of learning the hard lessons. The vig kept getting more impossible to pay.

By the second night, I started to hallucinate, which was the whole point. The first day was about seeing outward and I believed all my problems were outside of myself. The second day was about realizing my problems were all inside of me. The third day was about coming up with a plan – a real plan to take me to the next level and to solve my problems. It was about realizing that if I didn't get out of my own way, my life would continue to be shit.

I was in that circle to challenge myself, by myself and for myself. Part of the answer came as a child's voice in my head. Many years later, I actually met that child. But that's a story for another time.

It was a deeply emotional and profound seventy-two hours, digging deep and coming up with a new mental arsenal for my life. Walking out of that circle, covered in bug bites and the stench of my own body, I realized the next shower under the waterfall was going to be a different kind of cleansing.

\*\*\*

## A Trip Home, Getting Ripped Off, and Barter Day

When I left Jersey, I had the Ocean Avenue house under contract, and I needed to get back there for the closing. The cash from the sale would be enough to pay for the trip, buy some supplies, and bankroll another few months in Jamaica. So off I went to my old stomping ground.

While I was in town, I dropped in to see Hanze and find out why my stuff hadn't made it to Jamaica yet when he told me it had already been shipped, but when I got to the warehouse, there it was. When I confronted him about it, his excuse was that he wanted to be sure I was going to stay in Jamaica before he sent it. Apparently, a lot of people say they're going to stay at the hut, and then freak out when they see the living conditions.

Smelling bullshit, I went through my stuff and found that it'd been riffled through and some small (and expensive) items were missing. He insisted that the missing stuff was in another warehouse, but I didn't buy it, and it was never returned to me. This guy was supposed to be my friend, and he was clearly skimming my stuff. But I was booked on a flight back to Jamaica, so couldn't do anything about it.

When I got back to Jamaica, I told Dante, and he was rightly upset. We trusted this guy, had this big plan to build on his property, and he was screwing us. It was a bit of a wake-up call. I was a couple of months into something I'd planned to do for a year, and I was already looking in a different direction.

Before I left Jersey, I dropped into some local Italian stores to pick up victuals for Dante. I surprised him with some really good pastas and sauces, enough for everyone back in the bush. Some of the local dreads had never eaten Italian food before, and I knew Dante would make enough for everyone. That's just how he is. He shares everything.

I also picked up a surprise for my farmer friend, Howie. He had this funky old bike that reminded me of the ones we had as kids: parts from a bunch of old bikes, all held together with anything that would stick. He rode a lot, so I picked up a new bike for him. We later rode for hours at a time every chance we got, between Annatto Bay and Buff Bay, up and down every dirt road we could find. I wanted my friend to ride in comfort.

Whenever I made a trip to the States, I bought a bunch of stuff to take back to Jamaica, both as gifts for friends and as merchandise to barter with my neighbors. I bought lots of food, stuff like shirts from an artist in Jersey City that printed the same logo in bulk, and swag like fake Movado watches and Gucci sunglasses I picked up in Chinatown. The kids on Pump House Road loved when I came back because I brought everybody soccer balls, and we played for hours on the field at the base of the road. I'd have one of my friends pick me up at the airport with his jitney van, and they always knew they'd be able to chill out for the day. I paid them well for their time and made sure their families ate well for weeks with the stuff I brought back.

By the time I got home, it would be nighttime. The kids would make a line and carry my stuff up the hill to the hut. The next day was barter day. We'd make a big pot of porridge with oats and farina, coconuts and spices. It was real bush food that stuck to your ribs, and spliff cones would be lit everywhere.

Throughout the day, there was a steady stream of people bringing their wares up to the Hut to barter. We got fresh lobsters and fish from fishermen in exchange for baseball caps or sunglasses. Yard work was exchanged for watches. Farmers brought exotic fruits and vegetables, and elders brought food. It basically turned into a party of very cool people and their kids. We'd talk for hours while the kids exchanged coloring books and crayons, and the older kids happily played with their new soccer balls.

※ ※ ※

**Stuff That Happened and What I Learned**
A lot of unique and interesting things happened to me in Jamaica. A few of them weren't so great, but most of them ended up being positive and life-affirming. One of the things I love most about Jamaica is the raw natural beauty of the place and how it can catch you by surprise. The island, the people, and my memories of both are strongly formed by and around the sea. The pounding surf, the waterfall where I bathed, the unexpected and sometimes overwhelming rainstorms.

One day I was hanging out at a dry riverbed near the hut with Ronnie, the young daughter of one of my neighbors. It was still and silent, totally peaceful, perfect for contemplation and exploring. In a matter of moments, the silence was replaced with a furious roar as the riverbed filled with water and downed trees. I saw the terror in Ronnie's eyes, grabbed her, and leaped so high and fast up the side of the cattle fence on a stone embankment. It would have made an Olympian proud.

I'd seen the rampage of Hurricane Iniki when I was in Honolulu, and it was awe-inspiring and frightening. This was another kind of natural awesomeness, one that can swoop down and wash you away in a matter of moments. I have to think there's a reason we got out of that gully in time. If Ronnie remembers that moment now, I hope it isn't with the same terrifying intensity she must have felt that day. I haven't spoken to her since then, but I hope she's done some good in her life.

Saint Margaret's Bay in Portland had old, dilapidated columns and piers with the slabs partially under water. I used to imagine rebuilding the piers, replacing them with one beautiful project everyone could enjoy.

One beautiful day I went to hang out there and saw a kid walking along one of the docks holding a long line tied to his dog. When he reached the end of the dock, the dog jumped into about ten feet of water, and the kid led the dog through the surf back to shore. Then he led the dog back down the dock and did it again, over and over.

A lot of people would be really upset seeing this kid doing this to his dog. But I was curious what the fuck this kid was doing, so I made my way over toward him. When I got close to the dock, another dog blocked my path to the kid, put his head down, and growled. He stopped me dead in my tracks.

The kid came over to me and asked what I wanted, so I asked him what he was doing. He said his two dogs were his family, and he was teaching them to swim in the surf, so they could live through a flash flood.

It was an enlightening lesson about not judging people and situations based on what I saw. It taught me to question the witness and not rely on my own senses to tell me what's going on. It helped shape the way I now view events.

Dante and I often hosted visitors from the States for several days at a time. I'd rent a car for the week, pick them up at the airport, and drive them around to all the sights. I took a lot of folks out to hike and see the natural wonders of the island. I sometimes took them to the usual tourist spots where they could waste their money on cheap Chinese trinkets and get shitty service at an overpriced restaurant.

On one such occasion, I took our guest, Mary, to a lagoon on a brilliantly magnificent day. Howie came along, because he was my backpacking guide and knew great places to take the tourists. Mary went into the gift shop nearby, and Howie and I headed for the tables beside the lagoon with its sparkling, deep blue water lapping the shore to enjoy a couple of Cuban cigars.

When the waitress came by with only one menu, I asked for more. When Mary joined us, the waitress came back with only one more menu, and I asked her why. Because Howie had dark skin, she assumed he was the driver and said that drivers don't get served in that restaurant.

I didn't correct her incredibly rude assumption and decided to have a little fun. I asked Mary to pretend Howie was her husband and to order a shitload of beers and a bunch of food. The waitress was quite perplexed when it was made clear the black guy was Mary's husband, not the driver.

I snuck lots of beers from their order to help jack up the bill. When we were finished three hours later, I told Howie to take the car and Mary to the top of the hill, and I'd join them there. They casually left the restaurant, and I lit another Cuban.

The waitress came by with a ridiculously high check and put it by me.

I sat for a few more minutes while I wrote a note for the waitress. I explained that since I was the driver, and I wasn't served there, I wouldn't pay there. I put the note with the unpaid check and left. I never went back to that shithole place again.

One of my responsibilities was keeping our visitors safe, and I was hypervigilant about that. We had a tough and street smart Asian chick staying with us, and she didn't make my job easy. Food poisoning was at the top of the list of my concerns. She ate anything from fried fish to unwashed fruits and veggies and would drank water procured from who knows where. Since she was from the city, I thought the lack of amenities at the hut might be an issue. But sleeping on the floor, having no running water, and using the outhouse – she took it all in stride.

She was an attractive young lady, so naturally all my friends came around. Quirky Rastas, artists, and street hustlers all wanted to marry her, making ridiculous promises trying to capture her attention. She took it all with her great sense of humor and adventure, and her love of all people and experiences. We spent a lot of time walking the mountain roads and traversing rocky beaches, talking all the while.

When it was time for her to leave, we said our goodbyes. She told me she had a great time and was shocked to travel halfway around the world to Jamaica just to get a tour from a white boy from New Jersey. We both chuckled, then she gave me a hug and jumped on the market bus to Kingston.

✳ ✳ ✳

## The Market Bus, Hustlers and Pirates, and Men with Guns

Have you ever ridden on a market bus in a third world country? If you haven't, add it to your Bucket List because it's one of life's unique experiences. Sometimes I rode the bus to Halfway Tree in Kingston and back, and it's pretty much like you see in the movies.

People carry everything from chickens and goats, to big bags and boxes, to suitcases tossed on the top of the bus. It's standing room only, with twice as many people crammed in than it has seats for. To say it's packed with goods and people is an understatement. And the body odor can be mesmerizing in the heat.

I had a pretty typical start to my day – shower at the waterfall and a simple breakfast – and ended with a once-in-a-lifetime experience that I hope you never have to go through.

I caught the bus and stood in the back with a perfect view down the aisle. The ancient vehicle bucked and backfired with every punch of the clutch and shift of gears. Listening to the old engine and inhaling the exhaust was making me nauseous. I looked out the side window at the sheer cliff drop and thought this is the type of bus you read about in the papers when it slides off a cliff and kills a hundred people in a fifty-passenger bus.

Just as I was starting to seriously regret my choice of transportation, we were heading downhill, and it got more interesting. There was a little Indian man in the middle of the aisle with a four-foot wrench downshifting the transmission. I just closed my eyes and hoped for the best.

As we neared the Halfway Tree bus stop, I saw crowds of people, vendors hustling, and pretty much plain chaos. As you can imagine, it takes a bit of time to get all those people and all that cargo off the bus. I typically traveled with a specially rigged backpack with two machetes in cardboard scabbards strapped to the back with duct tape. I slung my pack and started on my way.

In rapid succession, someone grabbed me, then another, and then a third. They were cops who'd bum rushed me like I owed them money or something. One guy actually put a machine gun to my head, one grabbed the backpack off my shoulders, and one held me by the shirt. It happened so fast, I had no idea what was going on. I just knew it was a lottery I didn't want to play.

As they "escorted" me down an alley and through the back door of a building, they talked about me dealing and all kinds of other ridiculousness. The whole time, I thought the dude with the gun was going to pull the trigger, and that would be the end of that.

After about fifteen minutes of trying to break the ice by cracking jokes with these very intense individuals, I had to take my pants off and spread my cheeks. I kept thinking, "Who puts stuff up their ass?" I think they just did it to humiliate me, but at that time in my life, I couldn't feel humiliated about anything that happened to me. They did take my cash, which pissed me off, but I learned the importance of being nice to someone holding an automatic rifle to your head.

While those three "officers of the law" were clearly thugs, there were plenty of less terrifying thugs on the street. In the city, there was a guy "running" a section of a street, and he had his miniature foot soldiers following his orders and hustling anyone they could (mostly tourists).

One day when I was in Port Antonio with a friend of mine, one of these young paper soldiers came up to me and started the typical aggressive hustle. In the middle of this button-pushing performance, I heard a whistle from across the street. The kid immediately ran over to the whistler, who was sitting in a shop drinking a Red Stripe. After a brief conversation, the kid ran off to hustle someone else.

Being a curious cat, I approached the dread and asked what he'd said to the kid. He told me he'd just asked three questions. First, how many white brethren had the boy seen walking with a coolie today? The kid said one. Second, how many white boys did he see walking around with two machetes crisscrossed across his back? The kid said one. Third, did the boy think that the white boy knew how to use those machetes to defend himself? That's when the kid crossed the street to hustle someone else.

I thanked the boss for the respect and chatted for a few minutes. Turned out he knew some friends of mine from Boston Beach (the best place for jerk chicken). We went through the ritual of the fist bump and saying, "Everything is irie, mon." I went on my way, back to the road and the long walk to catch the market bus back to the hut.

Sometimes you expect someone to be fair and respectable and they turn out to be a hustler in disguise. Sometimes you expect someone to be a hustler and they turn out to be generous and kind. I had this upside-down experience while dealing with a rental car.

I was expecting a backpacker to visit for a few days, so I rented a car for the week. I drove to the trailhead of one of my favorite seaside spots for my morning bathing ritual rather than doing it at the waterfall near the hut. It was a bit of a trek from where I parked, and when I returned from my ablutions, I found one of the car's windows was shattered. I figured it could have been the intense heat or some kids messing around.

I had plenty of time to visit some friends and then go to the airport to exchange the rental. I already had a contract on the car, so I'd just swap cars. The problem was, in Kingston the usual rules don't apply.

The guy at the rental desk was a douche and insisted I had to close the original contract and open a new one for another car. I told him I didn't have much credit left on my card, and he assured me that wouldn't be a problem. He handed me the new contract and said he needed my credit card again. Why? He had to get approval from the credit card company. Why? When he closed out the original contract and credited my card, he also charged me for the broken window, which I had insurance for.

Bottom line was, the credit card company wouldn't approve the transaction because I didn't have enough credit left, so I couldn't get another rental car. I wanted to reach across the counter and strangle this guy who had assured me there'd be no problem. I was now stuck at the airport with a dead cellphone, no cash, and no credit on my card. It was close to sunset, and I had no way of getting home or contacting the guest, who ended up finding somewhere else to stay. I really lost my shit.

As shops and businesses were closing up, I asked every stranger walking by if I could get a ride home. People were grinning and laughing, and I realized I was the only white guy in a sea of Caribbean pirates and thieves. It was probably the most vulnerable I'd been in my life.

As the potential for getting a ride got slimmer and slimmer, I noticed a hustler out of the corner of my eye. He was one of those guys who could sell ice cubes to Eskimos. Not your average hustler, but a real pirate among thieves. You could practically see his virtual eye patch.

I approached him, and he said he was going to Port Antonio and could give me a ride to town. Well, that was a step in the right direction. I knew lots of people there who could get me to Pump House Road, so off we went. As his driver traversed through the Jamaican mountains, the pirate told me he had family in Windsor Castle who knew the story of the "Crazy White Man in da Bush." He meant Dante, whom everyone knew and loved.

To my surprise, instead of dropping me in Port Antonio, the driver took me to Pump House Road. I couldn't thank him enough and I ran up the steps in the pitch black, past the pump house to the hut to get him some cash for his trouble. Dante asked where the hell I'd been, and I hastily explained and took the cash he offered. I ran back down to the road, but the pirate and his car were gone. We'd talked about so many things, but we'd never exchanged names. After that day, I made a habit of giving people a ride if they need it. Some things you've just got to pay forward.

After a couple more months, my stuff still didn't come. I called it a loss and decided to leave Jamaica. I told Dante to get my stuff when it arrived and that it was his to do with what he wanted. I just wrote it off.

# CHAPTER 7

## Jersey City Once Again

**Returning to Nothing and Starting Over**

I returned to Jersey from Jamaica with two boxes containing just about all my worldly possessions. I had some stuff at my sister's house, but everything I'd left in "storage" in Jersey was shipped to Jamaica by Hanze after he was sure I was leaving. I felt like a putz for about a minute, but then thought about how much Dante would enjoy all the stuff. I felt a different kind of freedom. I'd left some Aloha Spirit there, and it felt damn good. Practically, I'd been fucked, but I chose to look at it as helping a friend.

I had no place to stay yet, so crashed at my brother and sister-in-law's house in Cliffside Park. My new home was my niece's bedroom – pink with unicorn pillows and mermaid sheets. Another one of life's humbling experiences, but the embarrassment only lasted about ten minutes. I was at another crossroads in my life, but I started turning left in my decisions rather than turning right like I was expected to.

From Cliffside Park, I could jump on a jitney bus and get to Jersey City without a car. Most days I had three newspapers in hand looking for houses again. I didn't care what it was, I would renovate anything and stay in the building while I worked on it. I still had some money from the Ocean Avenue house, but it wasn't much. I needed to hustle, so that's what I did.

One day I came home, and my brother remembered there'd been a postcard from Africa about a month before. It was from Jane, sent from one of the countries she visited. I gave her a call, and the conversation quickly went from "Hey, how've you been?" to "I want you to renovate my mom's kitchen." Little did I know, hooking back up with her would send me in another profound direction that would last two decades and is still going strong.

I met up with Jane at the house and met her mom, who was always "Auntie" to me after that. I thought she was the cutest thing ever. She spoke only Gujarati and talked to me as though I could understand her. After a while, I started understanding her meaning through body language and short sentences.

I worked on the house during the day while Jane was away, and soon met her sister, Rayna – in her early twenties, funny, sarcastic, and all street. We clicked immediately, and we talked all day while I worked.

Jane and I both loved hiking and walked all around Jersey City. We talked about business and real estate during our urban adventures. We dissected downtown and marked the neighborhoods we liked and started thinking about a real estate partnership.

✶ ✶ ✶

**Looking for Love**

I wasn't interested in dating at that time; I wanted to fall in love. I thought about it often as I met one girl after another. Jane teased me and told her friends to forget about me. I wanted to meet a woman I could talk to with my head lying in her lap. Someone to share thoughts with and have interesting conversations spanning from fart jokes to Socrates, from Ninja life to imperial societies, all the way to the vastness of the cosmos. And aliens. Bringing up aliens during a conversation can tell you a lot about a person and whether you want to hang around them.

One day I was tired and dragging my ass from plastering the hallway. While I was on a break, the doorbell rang, and Rayna said she was going out with one of her cousins. I'd been meeting all Jane's cousins and, believe me, each one was more beautiful than the last. But I'd never felt a connection with any of them.

This time, in walked this little ball of funky attitude in her Doc Martens, green khaki pants, and a strut like grunge had just arrived. I could only see her from the back, but her stride caught my attention. Of course, I asked Rayna some bullshit question just so I could get a better look at this elusive creature.

When my eyes met hers, I was floored. They were the most amazing I'd ever seen, exotic East Indian, and a gaze that would melt ice in the Arctic. After some idle chitchat and pleasantries, she went outside to wait for Rayna. I told Rayna that I was going to marry her cousin. On her way out the door, she laughed and said, "Easy, white boy, wrong flavor." I didn't care if I needed to be brown, black, green, red, or a transgender midget, I was up for the challenge.

About a month later, Jane invited me to a barbeque at a park in Central Jersey. Some of her aunts and uncles and cousins would be there. It wasn't going to be a big deal, and I knew the park was nice. Two things I love in life is nice parks and Indian food, so I hopped on the bus to Jane's house.

Indians are amazing in how they can pack so much shit and so many people into a little Corolla, just like a clown car. Jane's dad, Uncle, and I took the front seat, and Jane and Auntie took the back. Between them was a huge old potato chip tin filled with "chevdu," a sort of homemade Indian chex mix. On the floor at our feet were bags filled with vegetables, fruit, gallons of water, towels, napkins, and assorted cooking utensils worthy of a small restaurant. The trunk was half open, the hood held down by bungee cords, crammed full of enough tables and chairs to host a small party.

When we got to the park, there she was. Rayna'd told her cousin that I was chill and fun to be with, so Nishi and I hung out together. It was an afternoon of laughter, teasing, and sarcasm while we sat on a blanket just like a married couple. We took a nice walk together along with some cousins, and at the end of the day we exchanged numbers and parted.

*** * * ***

**Business (Not as Usual)**

After wrapping up the work on Jane's house, she and I set up a corporation and bought a building on Second Street using her credit cards. It had three apartments, so I'd live in one while I renovated the others. I took a salary of $350 per week, but little did I know that strategy would backfire. I figured out that instead of taking a large salary and draining our cash reserves, I could just pay my bills, vehicle, and daily expenses from the corporation and take the tax write-off. It was all about sweat equity up front, and cash on the back end when we refinanced or sold the house.

The hours were long – sometimes almost twenty a day – working on sheetrock, tile, and paint. Days turned into nights, and evenings blended into mornings. Since there was nothing to distract me from work, at times I didn't leave an apartment for days. Once I got one ready to rent, I moved into the next. Often tenants were moving in while I finished up some painting or caulking. Time was always in short supply.

I usually worked alone, but decided I needed some help. Hanging five-eighths inch sheetrock on the ceilings by myself sucked, even with the contraptions I made with two-by-fours. Dante had returned from Jamaica about a month after I did, so I called him up, and we became a team once again. We moved into the basement. There was already a toilet and a drain for a bathroom, so I knocked out a few walls, ran some copper pipe, hung some plastic, and we had a place to shower.

I was tired of cleaning up my financial messes but being an entrepreneur, it's part of the game. One day I got a notice from the State of New Jersey threatening to file a lien for taxes due on the restaurant I'd closed before leaving for Jamaica. I headed down to the tax office, scared. What the hell was a tax lien? I'd had a few run-ins with the IRS and always came up with some kind of payment plan, but this was something new.

The offices were definitely intimidating. I sat with the agent and we talked about the back taxes I owed and couldn't pay. I held my hands across the table wrist-to-wrist like I was going to be handcuffed. She explained that I didn't properly close out the paperwork on the restaurant. She asked if I ever owned ABC Construction, which I did, and said they were going to put a lien against that business, too.

Two hours and many, many, many pages signed later, I walked out thinking I'd dodged a bullet. That was a relief, but I was still scared. I really needed to get my financial house in order, so I started looking for a business accountant. I'd had accountants in the past, but I needed someone well versed in business, not just a bookkeeper.

※ ※ ※

## The First Street House

Jane and I bought another house on her credit cards, a three-story walk-up on First Street and Brunswick that needed a total renovation. I was back in the credit repair business and needed to start with a credit card and some small secured loans. Dad helped me by adding me to one of his cards, and Jane added me to the cards we used for materials. She was now working full time in the city to cover the bills while I renovated the house.

This project would test my will to the point of mental exhaustion. It wasn't very big but had to be completely gutted and divided into apartments. I was already used to working nights, so I worked during the day, napped in the afternoon, and continued stripping walls and removing the tin ceilings at night. Above the ceilings were piles of plastic jewelry collected by rats over the years, as well as inches of rodent shit all over the house. Underneath the house was quite a thrill – about a foot of old sewage that had been leaking from the pipes for decades.

Dante and I worked one floor at a time to the point of exhaustion. Uncle came to help us with the plumbing mechanics. With winter coming on, we got it down to the wood beams. The windows were all pulled out and there was no water or electricity. There was a two-story pile of debris accumulated in the backyard from all the shit we ripped out of the building.

Dante was sleeping at the Second Street house, but I stayed in the First Street house with nothing but a twin bed and the building exposed to the elements. No utilities, in the dead of winter, freezing my ass off. The walls in row houses are all connected, so I spliced an electrical line from my neighbor's house through the party wall. It was enough for an electric heater, which I kept next to the bed. While it was a welcomed relief from the cold, it was also a fire hazard if anything got too close to it. My fortitude was being tested daily. But roughing it in the bush of Jamaica prepared me for this challenge. I was up for it.

**Head Over Heels and Playing House**

> *She said we could get fat together.*
> *We did get comfortable.*

To make matters worse for myself, I fell in love. Not just in love, but head-over-heels in love with the most gorgeous girl I'd ever laid my eyes on. She hung out with me at the First Street house wearing a jacket, and we talked from early evening to early morning. When she left, I got a couple of hours of sleep, then started working again.

To say the relationship was intense is an understatement. We came from two very different backgrounds, both culturally and intellectually. She had the education, and I was the blue-collar guy. We remained friends for months, just enjoying one another's company. I always laughed when she left in her brand-new Lexus, while I was living in an abandoned and gutted house with no water and stolen electricity.

One night I asked her on a formal date and took her to Manhattan Bistro in Soho. Within a couple of weeks, we knew we would someday marry.

She moved into a little apartment across from the Second Street house, a cold-water flat from back in the day. There was no sink in the bathroom, just a claw-foot tub and a makeshift shower I'd put together from copper piping. I installed a small vanity sink, running pipes from the kitchen sink.

The only electrical outlet available for the TV was in the bathroom. Whenever anyone needed some privacy in there, we had to unplug the TV to close the door. The floors were so crooked, the TV on its wheeled cart would start rolling downhill across the apartment. It always cracked us up, and visitors laughed their asses off. At least she had water and electricity.

After about a year and a half, Nishi moved in with me into one of the apartments. As I finished one unit to rent out, we moved into the next one that needed renovating. I moved all our stuff while Nishi was at work, so she left one apartment in the morning and came home to another in the evening. We moved three times in two years. Our friends thought we were insane, but we were saving up to move to Florida, so the sacrifice was worth it. We were no different than any other entrepreneurs doing what needed to get done to be successful.

While we were cleaning out the First Street house, we turned the backyard into an oasis in the middle of the city. There was a twenty-foot stone wall at the back of the property, and I built custom wood fences on the sides. I made a huge wooden patio with benches along both ends that could sit at least twenty people. Dante and I filled up my old Mazda pickup a dozen times with used brick from an abandoned lot and used it to make a paved area from the back door to the patio the entire width of the house. We drilled holes in a metal garbage can, filled it with cinder blocks, put an old grill cover over it, and put it in the corner. We topped it off with charcoal and huddled around to keep warm during parties. We called it the Ghetto Grill. Once we finished the first floor, we had a kitchen and bathroom.

Our parties became legendary. Tiki torches and candles lit the back wall. Weed and wine flowed freely to everyone, from blue-collar guys renovating houses to banker kids working in lower Manhattan. They all knew we partied like rock stars til the early morning hours just about every weekend. Sometimes we heard what sounded like firecrackers, but when we heard the sirens we knew it was gunshots from the projects. We didn't care; nothing would get through that stone wall. We cooked and ate everything from salad to baked ziti, to sausage and peppers, to kebab chicken and lamb with a king crab boil. We ate well.

* * *

### Getting Married

Being in an interracial relationship has its problems, but we just saw each other for who we were as individuals. When we told our families and a few friends that we were getting married, they were surprised, to say the least. In the Hindu culture, the legal marriage ceremony is the formal engagement, and the religious wedding ceremony is held later. On the day we were married at City Hall, there'd been some sort of carnival for the kids the previous day. It hadn't been completely cleaned up, so the chambers where we took our vows had all kinds of clowns, paper balloons, and animal cutouts all over the walls. There was even a popcorn machine. Nishi had said she wanted to build a history between us before we had children, and this day was definitely one for our family annals, complete with high-wire acts and freakish sideshows.

For the religious ceremony, we decided on a destination wedding in Florida. We wanted to give living under some palm trees a shot, and this turned out to be the perfect opportunity to check it out.

# CHAPTER 8

## Tumbling Down and Filling Buckets

**Life in Jersey Changes**

In the early 2000s, downtown Jersey City was in the middle of a resurgence, with new buildings shooting up out of the ground almost too quickly to comprehend. Most of downtown was a construction site, with the next foundation going in before the last building was finished. I was remodeling the First and Second Street houses, and most of my friends were doing similar projects.

Our neighborhood had a character all its own. The gumbas stood around on the corner all day and squabbled about stuff they didn't know crap about. Just about any story they told was complete bullshit, but entertaining. One day I heard them arguing about the bobcat roaming the streets by the train tracks. One of the guys was like, "That's not a bobcat. The chink at the restaurant cut his fucking tail off while he was trying to cook 'im." These old guys all laughed their asses off with stogies hanging out of their mouths, just like juveniles talking about stupid schoolyard shit.

Nishi and I had plans to move to Florida and having our wedding down there. We were looking forward to the next phase of our life together, but it was going to be a bittersweet move. I was really going to miss the neighborhood, the feel of the place, and the friends I'd made.

So not only did we have the stress of planning and coordinating the Florida wedding from New Jersey, but we also had to sell off the two houses. Jane was buying me out of the Second Street house, and we were in the process of selling the First Street house. We had a lot of great memories from renovating those two houses, especially freezing my ass off during long winter nights and the Ghetto Grill parties. But we'd also be taking along with us to Florida the memory of one of the most impactful events of our lives.

* * *

**The Day**

As I stepped off the front stoop of the First Street house on a clear, beautiful morning, the corner of Brunswick and First Street was just starting to show signs of life. I had no idea that day would be seared into my brain like tuna and steaks on the Ghetto Grill. Suddenly there were police sirens wailing, and people were staring toward the Hudson River with looks of panic. I turned in that direction and couldn't believe my eyes. Smoke was billowing from the World Trade Center across the river. What the fuck?!?

I quickly headed to Second Street to get Nishi and told her to grab her camera. By the time we left the house to make our way down to the Hudson, the second plane had hit the second tower. It was complete pandemonium, with people screaming, "Oh, my God," "Jesus Christ," and "What the fuck?" A continuous stream of rescue workers, fire trucks, and ambulances were heading toward the river. They came in droves from nearby cities: Kearny, Newark, and Belleville, to name a few.

We stood on the corner completely in awe of what we were witnessing. It seemed like hours had passed, but it had been only minutes. Nishi asked if the building would fall. Based on what I could see and my construction experience, I figured the top of the building might fall over and damage the adjacent buildings. Just as I explained that to Nishi, we heard rumbles and police screaming through megaphones for everyone to get away from the river. With horror in our eyes and desperation in our hearts, we watched the first tower collapse into itself, replaced with billowing plumes of smoke.

I thought about the thousands upon thousands of people who worked in and visited those towers. With a shiver, I remembered my monthly ritual of visiting the World Trade Center to pay my credit card bill. I'd take the PATH train from the Grove Street Station wearing sweatpants and a t-shirt. I'd get off the train, go up the escalator, and grab a couple of newspapers and some sushi. I'd sit at the bottom of the escalators and watch all the people coming and going like they were a bunch of ants waiting in line to pick up some crumbs.

The screaming and crying around us were deafening. We all knew people who were there, people who wouldn't be coming home again. I just couldn't wrap my head around the idea that the tower was gone, with all those people in it. We learned that another plane had slammed into the Pentagon, and another went down somewhere in Pennsylvania. U.S. airspace was shut down nationwide for the first time in history, and all planes were ordered to land immediately.

Hundreds of us headed to Liberty State Park where we could see the remaining tower. We watched in horror as it also collapsed. We went down to the river where ferries were docking with the first survivors. People dressed in business suits covered in white ash—some bleeding, some being supported by others but all in shock—were disembarking. Countless numbers of volunteers were already there to help. The shock and disbelief on everyone's faces are etched into my mind forever.

As we talked with our neighbors throughout the day and into the evening, we realized that everyone knew someone who either had a close call—missed their train, was sick, took a day off to go shopping—or who would never come home again. We tried to call our family and friends, but the lines were overwhelmed by everyone else doing the same thing.

My friend George lived across from the First Street house and tended bar in Hoboken. His friend Adam had called him the night before. That afternoon and throughout the following day, George kept getting calls from Adam's phone, but Adam wasn't on the line. For some reason, his phone just kept pocket-dialing the last number he'd called. What a mind fuck. George was frantic thinking his friend was trying to call him from under the rubble, but I knew in my heart Adam was gone. George refused to give up hope and eventually started to lose it. We tried everything to console him, but nothing worked.

Two of the biggest towers in the world had collapsed, reduced to piles of burning rubble. I knew that I had to get there to help in any way I could. But how the hell was I going to get across the river? I ran scenarios through my head and decided that the next day, I'd get there somehow.

✳ ✳ ✳

**Getting There and the Importance of Buckets**
The day after the towers fell, I pulled on some Tyvek coveralls and duct-taped the legs into my work boots, so nothing could get in. My body couldn't breathe, but at least I'd be protected. But how was I going to get to Manhattan with all the bridges and tunnels closed? I had to get there to help, and the only way was by boat. I grabbed my respirator and headed to the river. I knew it would be a challenge, but I was up for it. A least I thought I was.

Two hours later, I was on a boat heading across the river toward Battery Park. Everyone was apprehensive and silent, all thinking the same thing: What the hell am I doing? Trying to pull up somewhere to disembark, the National Guard refused to let us get off and told us to go back to Jersey City. We all wanted to help, but today wasn't our day. Some guys were relieved, and some were disappointed.

As the boat turned back toward Jersey, I looked at the still-smoldering remains of the towers and saw an abandoned baby carriage on the river walkway. I took a photo and tried to imagine the sheer terror of the person who grabbed the baby out of that carriage and ran like hell.

When we got back to Jersey City, we all volunteered to help the responders who were returning from Ground Zero. There were hundreds of people behind the barricades, all cheering and applauding the guys who were getting off the boats. We gave them food and water and wrapped wet towels around their necks. I'd never seen such blank stares as I did on those returning men, and I knew I needed to be across the river helping. Most of my friends were in construction, and those who returned said they'd never seen anything like it before. I was ready to go.

The next day, the second day after the attacks, I donned my Tyvek, grabbed my respirator, and headed back to the river. When I got to the launch, I couldn't believe the number of trucks loading pallets upon pallets of buckets onto the boats. I wondered what the buckets were for.

The routine of the previous day repeated. A boat pulled in, guys disembarked, volunteers gave them food and water and wiped them down with wet towels, and the people behind the barricades cheered. I easily got past the barricades in my construction gear. An exhausted guy came off the boat, and I sat him down and gave him some water. When he put his hardhat down, I picked it up. Another guy was changing his shirt, so I grabbed his vest and wrote my name and telephone number on the back with a Sharpie. These guys weren't going back, but I was going to get there one way or another.

Behind me, I heard, "Hey, you! We're one short. Get on the boat." Before I knew it, I was on a boat with about fifteen guys and about a thousand buckets. Someone said that some of the guys at Ground Zero had been there for two days and cautioned us to stifle our shocked reactions when we got there. They were at their breaking points, and the last thing they needed to hear from a fresh batch of guys was, "Oh, my God. This is unbelievable." We all knew we had to keep our shit wired tight, but nothing could have prepared me for what I was about to see.

We disembarked at the pier by the towers and unloaded the buckets. There were supplies everywhere. At the dock and lining the streets were dozens of pallets of water and juice, construction equipment, generators, and just about anything needed for the job at hand. We each grabbed a stack of buckets to take wherever they were needed. I carried about twenty, but still had no idea what they were for.

There were people everywhere—firemen, cops, construction workers, engineers, doctors, nurses, and people looking for loved ones. There were guys taking a break and others starting a shift. Food lines, water lines, and tables of medical supplies filled the pier.

Someone pointed me in the right direction, and I started making my way. I went through the Winter Garden Atrium, and half of the roof was gone. I walked past restaurants with food still on plates ready for hungry customers who wouldn't be coming back. Doors were blown off hinges and girders hung precariously from the ceilings. I saw black bags all piled one on top of another and was pretty sure what they were. A huge picture window had blown out, and I was able to step over a knee wall to the outside. I couldn't see very well carrying all those buckets, so I set them down and just stood there in awe.

I couldn't wrap my head around the leveled buildings and huge piles of debris. It stretched for blocks in all directions, including on top of the fire trucks and police cars. Suddenly I heard an ear-piercing horn, followed by men screaming, "RUN!" We all bolted back toward the river. I heard a rumble from underground, and then a section of a building collapsed right on top of my buckets. That was my introduction to Ground Zero.

A group of ironworkers was looking for guys who knew how to burn steel. I learned how to handle a torch back when I was working with the Greeks, so I volunteered. Let's go cut some steel, I thought. I had no idea what to expect.

I ended up in a construction bucket with two other guys, being hoisted by a crane about six stories up to cut steel off the side of a building. I was sick to my stomach. I'd never been afraid of heights, but I was in a three-by-six-foot half-open construction cage and I could see the destruction all around.

After an hour and a half, I had to get down. The guys with me knew I was starting to lose it, but they also knew I was keeping my shit together. These ironworkers went up in buckets and cut steel all day long for a living; we all knew I'd be more useful on the ground. One notable thing about construction workers is their sense of humor. Their breaking-my-cherry jokes were kind of funny.

Back at the staging area, I got some water and a couple of smokes, and then joined a group starting a bucket line. The debris was so tangled and intertwined, we literally had to pick out one piece at a time. The bigger chunks were passed down the line from one guy to the next, while the smaller stuff was collected in a bucket. Once the bucket was full, it went down the line and was replaced by an empty bucket. When the guy at the front of the line needed a break, the next guy in line took his place, and on it went. We were all standing on burning steel and collapsed buildings, and time seemed to pass very slowly. I remember thinking, "I'm standing on top of the World Trade Center."

After a couple of hours, I was at the front of the line taking my turn with the digging. Everything was covered in white ash. For the most part, everything looked like everything else, but some pieces had familiar shapes: a purse, a wallet, part of a telephone, or a shoe that wasn't empty.

When the piercing sound of a fighter jet flew over, everyone cheered. But I thought that he was two days too late. I took a break and went to a staging area where some guys were being counseled, while others prayed or joked around to break the emotional intensity. They came from all walks of life: firemen, cops, construction workers, doctors, veterans from the Korean, Vietnam, and Gulf wars, all crying and comforting each other. I listened to some of the guys' stories, then headed back to work.

Somebody was looking for someone to run a Bobcat, so I volunteered. For hours I was clearing nothing but ash and papers. Piles and piles of the shit. I was really glad I brought my respirator because I was completely covered with ash. I was getting tired by then, and honestly, I was done. I was played out mentally and physically, and I wanted to get home, so I headed for the pier.

I went back on a boat with about ten other guys, all of us completely wiped out. Everyone had a weird look on their faces, something I hadn't seen before. Kind of a glazed "holy shit" look. One of the Coast Guard guys laughed, saying we were probably going to sink the boat from all the weight hanging on us. It was actually kind of funny because the nose of the boat was up in the air from the load of us in the back.

Arriving at the dock on the Jersey side was déjà vu. People gave us water and put wet rags around our necks while onlookers applauded. It was a weird reality shift. I knew these people had no clue the sick shit we'd just witnessed on the other side of the river.

Going back to Nishi was weird. It was rather emotional because she didn't know what I'd been through but had some ideas. The smells of the pile and the white dust covering me made way for a tight embrace, one I'll never forget. When I think about that event in my life, I just think about the hug I got from Nishi. Tight and comforting. A special tenderness shared.

✳ ✳ ✳

### Getting Past Security and Poignant Silence

I needed some time to process what was going on around me, and what I'd seen and experienced. During the day, I continued getting the houses ready to sell. We were closing on the First Street house in a few days, and then going down to Florida to firm up our wedding plans the following week. I realized that I had options when many other people's dreams were now shattered. It was a humbling experience.

Sometimes I went down to the river and watched the smoke billowing toward the heavens or watched from the

Starbucks on the corner at night. I just could not get over the way the world had changed in one morning. Then I remembered that the rest of the world had been suffering attacks day in and day out for decades. Why should we be any different?

I knew I needed to help one last time before I left Jersey. My second day at Ground Zero was five days after the attacks. This time, I took a train to Christopher Street and walked down the West Side Highway, and the scene became surreal. Pictures of missing loved ones filled the fences and walls. Fire trucks from cities and states all over the country, mobile police command centers, and portable construction trailers lined the streets, stretching for blocks and blocks.

There were people holding prayer candles and comforting one another on the sidewalks, hugging, crying, praying, and applauding the guys leaving the site. As I got closer to Ground Zero, there were fewer people and more barricades. Nearer the site, it looked like an organized event.

There were portable fences now, and the gates were protected by guys with machine guns. The military presence in the staging area was overwhelming, like something out of a Rambo movie. Even though I had my vest, hardhat, and Tyvek coveralls, they didn't want to let me in. I told them I'd just left for a couple of hours, and there was a guy waiting for me to run a Bobcat. I told the guard that I was just going one last time, and he said that tighter security was the new protocol. After a couple of minutes of going back and forth, he finally relented. I signed in and now had a badge. I was officially a Ground Zero contractor.

I headed back to the area I worked the first time. I knew those guys I'd worked with before would be staying until they reached their breaking point, but no one looked familiar. The site was packed with food carts and vans, stands with clothes, boots, and emergency equipment, and just about anything else you can imagine would be needed to deal with something of this magnitude. We just picked up what we needed and went to work.

For some reason, I thought that a lot of the site would already be cleaned up. Looking back, I don't know why I thought that because it was absurd. This was going to take months, even with the new level of organization that was apparent. And it looked like specific companies were starting to take over.

I joined a bucket line, but this time it was a bit of a different experience. I could actually feel the heat of the beams and debris I was standing on. It took me a while to realize that the soles of my boots were becoming pliable, slowly melting around my feet. It took only a few hours before the soles of my feet got really hot and I needed new boots. I asked someone where I could get some, and the guy just pointed over to the pier and told me to go shop at the mall.

After I found new footwear, I was one in a long stream of people moving in and through the medical tents. Guys were getting hurt by the minute, mostly cuts, broken bones, and dust and debris in their eyes. Earlier in the day, like hundreds of other guys, I got debris in my eyes that needed to be flushed out. The doctor who treated me was fast and efficient, and after some chitchat, I was on my way back to the line. This time, I was treated for the blisters that formed on my soles. They packed my new boots with lots of gauze to make it more comfortable. It felt like I was floating on air.

Walking back to the bucket line, I suddenly heard a loud "boom" and what sounded like an ear-piercing missile shoot overhead. One of the oxygen or acetylene tanks in one of the buildings got hot enough to blow. To say I was shitting my shorts is an understatement. Even though I wasn't that close to the sound, it was definitely frightening. A couple of guys got hurt and needed medical attention. Not for the first time, I wondered what the fuck I was doing there. The media broadcast it, and later I found out Nishi was frantic, thinking one of the injured men was me.

They'd moved in heavy equipment by now to pick up and move huge pieces of debris, with the bucket lines coming in behind them to get the smaller stuff. Watching the big machinery expertly lift partial sides of a metal building overhead, and the different hardhats and bosses everywhere, it seemed like those guys must have been union contractors. Giant trucks were lined up waiting for their loads, all in a hurry so they could dump the debris and get back to pick up another load. I wondered if they were getting paid by the truckload, and I was sickened to think of companies making a profit off this tragedy while there were so many volunteers giving their all for free.

The Bobcat guys were still around, so I jumped on a machine to give my feet a break. At least that's what I thought. After hours on the pedals clearing paths so stuff could be hauled out, the blisters on my soles were open. My feet were killing me, but I thought, "Just a few more hours, and I'm out of here."

By then the work had taken on a different kind of sadness. Instead of searching for survivors, we were looking for remains to give to the families, or at least some DNA that could be matched up. But even with all the chaos of machinery and people spread out over several blocks, if someone thought they heard something coming from below, everything immediately came to a grinding halt. I swear you could hear a pin drop as everyone strained to listen for the smallest sound of life. It was amazing to experience the absolute chaos of the crews cleaning up, and then the absolute silence of the crews straining to hear a possible survivor.

I was there when someone was found. What happened next woke the humanity in me and all of those around me. The body was placed on an EMT board, wrapped in an American flag, and ever-so-slowly, with the greatest respect, was carried down the line, passing from one person to the next. Over seventeen years later as I write this, remembering that scene still brings tears to my eyes. That was my breaking point. I wasn't as tough as I thought I was, and I needed out.

I walked back to the chapel where a lot of guys went for comfort. I just needed to hold my face in my hands and let it all out. I didn't want people to think I was weak, but I was surrounded by all these tough guys just hugging each other, crying, and telling sick jokes just trying to put their minds right. When the anger set in, I had to find a boat back across the river.

I found a small spot to take it all in. In my mind, I said my goodbyes and wished everyone well, then limped back to the pier. I was physically exhausted and mentally fatigued, and I just wanted to hug my girl. Coming off the boat, we were all again greeted by volunteers there to help us get cleaned up, and lines of people along the barricades applauding.

I had nightmares for years after that. One in particular played out nightly. In my dream, I was at the front of the bucket line and picked up something that looked like a scalp with long hair. Hell, it could have been a piece of rug, but in my dream it was a scalp. What haunted my nights and echoed through my waking hours was not being able to put a face to what I'd discovered—a faceless scalp in the thoughts of an emotionally distraught man.

Now years later, and although the emotional impact of those days has been tempered by time and other significant life experiences, the physical effects have lingered. When we think of First Responders, most of us generally think of firefighters, EMTs, law enforcement, etc., and of the fight to get them the medical and psychological care they need to recover from that horrific event.

But I also remember all the guys who managed to get themselves to Ground Zero with no idea of what to expect, no experience, and no training but did what needed to be done. Years later, I developed breathing problems and unexplained pain that affected every aspect of my life, something that the doctors weren't able to diagnose or treat. Finally, in 2017, I was diagnosed with a carcinoid tumor and had two-thirds of my right lung extracted.

I think often of all those other guys who showed up. I wonder how they're doing, and I wish them well.

✳ ✳ ✳

## Closing Up Shop and Getting the Hell out of Dodge

Two days later, I was supposed to close on the First Street house. I found out the buyer was one of those near-miss people who'd been at the Towers the day they fell, and he was so distraught he couldn't make it to the closing. Who could blame him? The closing was pushed back, and the buyer gave his lawyer power-of-attorney to finish the deal. When I asked the lawyer about the buyer, he made some smug remark about us being pushy about closing, and that his client couldn't come because he was dealing with his emotions. Funny, so was I.

It really made me think about business in a different way. There are tragedies every day, and yet business never stops. Currency flows down all the rivers in life, and there's always someone there looking to make a profit from other people's grief. It sometimes leaves me shaking my head in disbelief thinking about the cruelties of the business world.

In the midst of all of this, we had to wrap up our wedding plans and our move to Florida. We'd just witnessed some of the craziest things humans can do to each other, and now I had to get on a plane to Florida. To say I was nervous would be an understatement. Nishi was already there, and I missed her terribly. I was also worried because brown people were now the new target. Rednecks didn't know the difference between Muslims, Hindus, and Sikhs, and they probably didn't care.

We had the venue settled and would have our wedding on the beach (or so I thought). The cake and music vendors were in Florida, but I was still coordinating flying the DJ from Atlanta and the florist and all the flowers from Hawaii. Stress was high and tension even higher. Like any wedding, you want to be sure everything is perfect. I flew down to Florida, flew back to Jersey, and then drove back down with all our shit in under a week's time. Very trying times, indeed.

# CHAPTER 9

## The Same Old Stuff, Only Different

**A New Life in a New State**

We left New Jersey on the heels of tragedy and in the middle of coordinating our Florida wedding from 1,200 miles away. To say that it was completely insane would be an understatement. But we were looking forward to our new life with great anticipation. We'd get married, settle into our new condo in Ft. Pierce, and get started making our fortune in real estate.

Our wedding day came, and like a lot of weddings, whatever could go wrong did. The cake people thought the ceremony was the following week, so we had to sort that out. We were flying the DJ in from Atlanta, and the flowers from out of town. When the audio guys arrived at the venue with all their equipment, there was no one there to help them unload. They were threatening to leave with all their stuff, so I left the hotel with Jane's dad and husband to help them set up. On my wedding day. And, it was really windy, so our beach wedding ended up being a parking lot wedding.

But our biggest concern was security. In the immediate wake of 9/11, tensions were high. Anyone with brown skin could be mistaken for a Muslim, which in some redneck areas of the South could be dangerous. My brother's friends were in law enforcement and brought their weapons.

Finally, everything got sorted out. All our Indian family and guests were dressed in Indian formal wedding attire and looked amazing. Now it was time for me to get dressed. The kurta I wore was a really cool, long white jacket embroidered down the sides with matching pants. Then there were the genie shoes and a box. What the hell was in the box? An Aladdin hat. Alright, who cares. If I had to wear it, I'd wear it.

As I was getting dressed in the venue's bathroom, I met a man who was also dressing for the wedding. We introduced ourselves, and he turned out to be my future father-in-law's best friend. I said, "I'm Craig, the groom," and next thing I knew we were hugging in the bathroom in our underwear. Suddenly the door opened, and a waiter walked in. He stopped in his tracks, looked at us, turned around, and walked right back out.

My biggest fear was leaving the bathroom and bumping into the only person on the planet I didn't want to see me at that moment. Sure enough, there he was, my brother, and he immediately started laughing. Not just laughing, but belly laughing with tears rolling down his face. All I could say was, "Thanks, dick." I swear, I heard him say, "No! Thank you!"

After the wedding, Mark enlarged a photo of me in my wedding attire complete with Aladdin slippers and hat, framed it, and hung it in his basement office. He told all my nieces' and nephews' friends that if anyone fucked with his family, he'd send Aladdin after them. Obviously, anybody crazy enough to wear that outfit was bound to be dangerous.

I was all decked out for the ceremony, the guests were assembled, but where was the bride? We'd had a beach party the night before, but Nishi didn't go because she was getting her mehndi (henna) done. Most of the young adults were hung over and had to wait two hours for the (un-hungover) bride to appear. Two hours in a tent with the hot Florida sun beating down and clouds rolling in.

Despite the challenges, it was a great day.

✳ ✳ ✳

## Big Plans and Card Games

After the wedding and honeymoon, we got to work. We had a plan: to become financially free in the shortest amount of time possible. We had an LLC to hold properties, and an "S" corporation to manage them. I hit the streets and went crazy shopping for handyman specials, owner-financed properties, lease options, no-money-down deals, assignments, and "subject-to" properties. I even took over some no-qualifying, fully-assumable loans that really pissed off the banks. You see, if the seller has been paying the mortgage for, say, twenty years, most of the interest has already been paid. When we took it over, we were mostly paying principle and building up equity.

Just like in Jersey, I did my research at the courthouse where I met other qualified investors looking for properties. I met several investors this way who have become good friends. We found people who were in default and bought properties in neighborhoods where people didn't want to buy. I was part of a group of about ten guys all doing the same thing. Our little group of investors went into a few connecting neighborhoods, bought up about 200 houses, and fixed them up. We literally changed the landscape in these areas.

Once we got possession of a property, I redid the bathrooms and kitchen and installed central air conditioning. We'd buy a $30,000 house in an $80,000 neighborhood, put $15,000 - $20,000 into it, end up with $30,000 in equity, and then either sell it or rent it. The single-family units were the best because those renters usually stayed in a house longer than in an apartment because it feels more secure. They also mostly don't want to become buyers, so that's another reason they stay longer than apartment renters.

I worked tirelessly, learning and teaching myself how to be my own bank and succeeded in becoming a deadbeat. That term might confuse the average person. It's not someone who doesn't pay their debt; it's someone who pays their debt in full and on time. The banks make their money on interest and fees, so if you're not paying them the vig, you're a deadbeat in their eyes.

Everything I learned about going broke, I was also learning about getting rich using the banks' money. We were buying houses using credit cards and lines of credit as the down payment, then paid them down once we refinanced. We worked our way up to dozens of cards and hundreds of thousands in credit. We never missed an opportunity to purchase property because we always had the down payment. We used credit cards, personal lines of credit from family members who would earn more interest from us than if they'd kept their money in a bank or took out second mortgages on one of the other properties.

We did this over and over again, building up a portfolio of properties. We did most of the work ourselves, so back to sleeping on the floor and napping in the hallway. I listened to all those real estate courses and no-money-down tapes night and day as I painted or tiled a unit til three in the morning. It was quiet then, and I could work uninterrupted, often with Nishi right beside me tiling or grouting.

When we finished or rented out a house, we celebrated by going on a cruise or flying to one of the Caribbean islands. When we got back, we worked on another house. We did this for three years, day in and day out. One year we took twelve trips.

I enlisted the help of a guy I met through our condo association who worked at the local firehouse. He had all the skills and experience an investor could ask for—plumbing, electrical, and air condition systems. We became fast friends. The best part about Marty was he liked to work odd hours, even weekends. When a job was done, we left his payment in one of our shoes in the carport. If it was a big payment, I'd leave it in my shoe; smaller payments went into Nishi's shoe. It became a running joke between us.

Marty also introduced me to a gentleman who became invaluable in our plan of financial freedom. John was like no other accountant I'd ever met. He had a great personality in addition to intelligence. He still helps keep our financial house in order, and he's also a great friend.

I was one of those guys who ordered the tapes and CDs from the 4 a.m. infomercial TV guru, and I applied everything I learned. I acquired a couple dozen properties using owner financing and other techniques I'd learned, so it was pretty cool when a film crew called and asked if they could film my testimonial. Their questions were pretty basic, but I was more into the publicity aspect of the whole thing. I asked them more about their equipment than they asked about our success. I made sure not to sign the releases, and what I learned about publicity helped me in the coming years.

## The Joys of Being "The Man"

I was the greatest landlord in the world, until I wasn't. After we moved into the house we'd bought for ourselves, we rented out our condo, which had some sentimental value for us. Our tenants were a guy and his girlfriend, and they seemed okay enough. I never ran credit checks on potential tenants because I know everybody has problems, but I did ask for their second-to-last employer and second-to-last landlord as references.

A lot of landlords don't think through checking references. If you call me up and ask about the guy who just moved out of my building, I'll give you a stellar reference even if he was an asshole, just so he's no longer my problem. But the previous landlord is more likely to be unflinchingly forthright because he's got no reason not to be.

Anyway, back to this gem of a tenant. Everything worked out well for a few months. They paid their rent, and the guy was respectful; I was always "Mr. Sotkovsky." Then one day I got a call from the girlfriend letting me know they were splitting up and she was moving out. I thought, "Great, I just inherited a bachelor."

The first month after she left, he gave me a story about how he had some problems and would be late paying his rent. After a couple of weeks, it got ugly. When I called him up to ask for the rent, he threaten to shoot me.

Then, one day out of the clear blue, he walked up my driveway. I met him outside, and we got into a heated discussion. That's when I became his "dawg" and he called me a racist and said I didn't like black people. I asked him why I would have rented to him in the first place if I didn't like black people, but he didn't have an answer for that. You sometimes run into stupid people in this business, people who love to cause problems just because they can't pay their rent.

Another tenant I nicknamed "Napoleon." I didn't mind this guy much because he had this funny ritual. He was an agricultural worker, about four-foot-six, and he loved to drink. I generally gave all my tenants a week's grace period before making a personal visit to collect. Every month I visited Napoleon to collect my rent, only to be told I was greedy and unfair. Napoleon would be drunk, cuss me out, give me fifty reasons why I was an asshole for trying to collect my rent, and threaten to kick my ass. The next day, without skipping a beat, he'd call me up to apologize and explain that he had a drinking problem. He always made me laugh.

Then there were the Cooks. They needed to move into a place fast, and I happened to have a nice apartment available on three-quarters of an acre with a creek running through it. Going through their paperwork and checking their references, I found out I knew their boss, who ran a gas station and convenience store. He gave them a stellar reference, and they moved in on a Friday. On Saturday, someone found out where they lived, someone they'd screwed over years before in a drug deal. They went to their employer's gas station and robbed it, and just took off in the middle of the night. The next day, the sheriff's department called about a problem at the duplex, so I went to check it out. The Cooks were gone, but all their stuff was still there. They'd left fast, leaving behind birth certificates, family photos, books, furniture, you name it, which I had to store for months. Going through their stuff, we found a cookbook for making crack.

    I'll remember the Architect's scam until the day I die. I got a call from a girl who was probably about twelve years old. Mom, dad, daughter, and grandma were all moving up from Fort Lauderdale, and this little girl was the translator for the family. Dad was apparently an architect, and all their paperwork and references checked out. Later I found out all the paperwork and references were bogus. Even the companies I'd called were fictitious.

    These folks put ads in all the local Mexican and Latin American newspapers offering to bless your money, cure your cancer, and fix just about anything that ails you. A lot of Hispanics in the area hated banks, especially the day laborers and pickers, and the Architect preyed on these people. He even went so far as to put the address in huge numbers on the front of the house, so their marks could easily find it.

They moved in in October and were late on December's rent. I arranged to pick it up on a Tuesday. When I arrived, the cops were there along with about fifty people on the lawn all crying and screaming. They started asking me a bunch of questions, but I had no idea what the Architect and his family had been doing. Inside, the house was decorated beautifully for Christmas with presents under a tree. But the wrapped boxes were all empty. The whole thing was staged. I later found out they'd taken hundreds of thousands of dollars from the Hispanic community and took off with the money along with my rent.

The hardest part of the whole thing was trying to clean up all the fingerprint powder used throughout the house. It was everywhere, but not a single print was found. Before they took off, the family had washed everything and left everything wet, so there were no fingerprints left to track them down.

* * *

## An Endeavor of Coffins and Saints

Real estate wasn't the only business we got into. A buddy took a vacation to Turks and Caicos, and when he got back we talked about investing in real estate and business ventures on one of the island. He'd met a guy with a store who was interested in importing merchandise from America, and real estate development was booming. So Nishi and I booked a trip to Turks and Caicos to check it out.

Providenciales is a pretty typical Caribbean island, laid back with hustlers everywhere. We met my buddy's contact at a restaurant and liked his warm, hospitable demeanor. He took us around to all the big stores looking at the types of merchandise we could import and sell below current retail prices, mostly tools and clothing. We returned home with a price list and some research to do.

I found out that our local Fort Pierce pier had a customs office and a broker/shipper. Wouldn't you know it, one of the first places they went to was Turks and Caicos. I subscribed to all the import/export magazines and learned about drop-ship cargo and second-hand apparel. I compared prices for tools and name brand clothes and corresponded with our guy on the island to figure out what we wanted to ship.

It would be an easy profit. I could buy a circular saw for $35 and ship it to my guy in Turks and Caicos who could sell it for $90. After shipping, taxes, and duty, we'd split a $40 profit just for buying something from one part of the world and selling it in another.

I'd been making frequent business trips to Georgia, and on my way back from one of the trips I stopped at one of the outlet malls. I bought about $1,500 worth of shirts, pants, and the stuff off the bottom of the racks. Odd colors didn't really matter because everything had some kind of name brand emblazoned across the chest or pocket. Back home, I went to Home Depot and bought all kinds of cheap drills, circular saws, levels, and other tools.

When I'd been touring construction sites on the island, I noticed no one had job boxes – a secure but mobile place to lock up your tools so they don't get stolen. So, I bought job boxes and loaded the tools into them. It would make shipping nice and tidy, and the boxes could be sold separately on the other end.

I filled out the paperwork for the shipping and had already gone over the pricing with my guy on the island. I even bought him a portable car power washer as a gift to celebrate our new venture. There was a parking lot next to his store where he ran a car cleaning service and I figured some new equipment would be a nice "thank you" for giving me the opportunity to make some money in Turks and Caicos.

Once I had all the details about delivery dates and such, I faxed him all the paperwork. He was praising me and Jesus for giving him the opportunity to make money with an American partner. It was nice to be appreciated. We were in contact at least twice a week to coordinate everything. The deal was that as soon as he started selling the stuff, he'd start sending me money to cover the cost of purchasing everything I'd bought and shipped. I figured I'd see how this shipment went, and if it went well and generated a profit, I'd start sending him containers full of tools and clothing.

I gave it about two weeks for the shipments to get to him and for him to set everything up in his store. When I didn't hear back, I didn't think anything was odd. After the third week of not hearing from him, I sent an email that simply said, "Hey, what's going on?" No response.

I had plenty of responsibilities in Florida keeping me busy, so I let it ride for a while longer. After another week, I sent another message and got no response. I sent him ten emails and left a dozen voicemail messages over the course of four weeks and didn't get a single response. I thought to myself, "Since nobody's emailing me or returning my calls, I'll send a scathing email." And that's what I did. I informed my partner that Jesus would not appreciate how he was treating his partner in the U.S.

The next day I got an email from the guy's wife telling me that all the goods were sold, but they couldn't do anything with the "coffins" I'd sent them, meaning the job boxes. I asked her where the money was, and she informed me I wouldn't be getting any money and that *I* had wasted *their* time.

I chalked up this episode to nearsightedness and greed on my part. If it seems too good to be true, then odds are, it is. I never went back to Turks and Caicos. I figured I might end up in jail.

∗ ∗ ∗

**The Measure of Success**
One day, my buddy Mike called and said he was back in town after visiting Europe. This is a guy I truly love talking with, so I went over to his house even though it was 10:00 p.m. When I got there, he was sitting on the hood of his truck smoking a cigarette, so I ask him what was up. Turns out the power company shut off his electricity for lack of payment while he was out of the country. There we were, sitting in the dark talking about putting together 200-, 300-, 500-thousand-dollar deals while we were waiting for the power company to come turn his lights back on.

You're probably thinking, "Power companies don't send someone out at 10:00 p.m. to turn someone's lights back on," and you're right about that. Mike had gotten to the company's office to pay his bill just before it closed. Somehow, he talked the shift manager into sending someone out to restore his electricity in the middle of the night.

That's the power of the ability to bullshit taught only at the School of Hard Knocks. Mike has a college education, but he also has street smarts, practical experience, and balls. He was only twenty-eight years old at the time but still managed to get shit done. He was broke then, and now he's a millionaire.

Do your kids know practical life skills like balancing a checkbook? Can they read a recipe, shop for the ingredients, and cook a meal from scratch? Jump the dead battery in your car? Read an opinion on a blog and come to their own conclusion? Give your kids everything, and they'll end up with nothing. Teach them to fish, and they'll eat for the rest of their lives.

Part of what we considered success was the ability to travel. My buddy Dread was raised on Union Island, and we wanted to see where he grew up. So we embarked on a journey that took us to Union Island, part of St. Vincent, and the Grenadines, and we brought Dread along, so he could visit his home. We flew out of Atlanta International and landed in Barbados. There we hopped on one of those very small thirty-person prop planes that would take us to Union Island. It was rather old, and the seats reminded me of being in an excavator – very tight, with a leg bar by your feet, and your ass could feel the metal bar through the seat cushion.

I'm telling you, it was a scary ride but had one of the most beautiful views. My favorite scenes are of the ocean – the many colors spanning from deep blue to turquoise all the way to the beaches. We saw the island from the air, and I was shocked by how small it was. I wondered how we would land. After circling the island, we came over one of the majestic peaks on this little oasis that's been dubbed "Little Tahiti of the Caribbean." As the plane touched down, my jaw dropped at the beauty.

Seeing the smile on Dread's face was priceless. He was home, even if just for a quick visit. He'd told me stories about his childhood, and now I got to see it through his eyes. Dread wandered off to his family's house while Nishi and I checked into the little hotel. It was literally on the runway, but the front view of the beach was breathtaking.

While we were there, we heard the story of this guy who had a crazy vision. Because there were so many conch shells around, he decided to take them out to the reef, make a little island out there, and open a restaurant on it. Everybody thought he was crazy, but now he's world-famous. We had a fabulous meal at this unique dining spot, and the rum punch still has me drunk thirteen years later. Lesson learned: don't ever lose hope of seeing your dreams fulfilled.

Leaving this tiny island post-9/11 was hysterical. At the airport, we went through the typical security check. The customs guy stood at the metal detector and waved me through. I turned around to watch my wife come through and noticed that the metal detector wasn't even plugged in. I belly laughed at this guy waving people through in such an official manner, knowing full well it wasn't doing anything. I guess they just wanted to make their guests feel secure in their little airport.

We were able to take trips like this one often, and that led us to think about getting our own plane. I was looking at a Hawker jet and planned to build a hangar that would house it along with a small jet and a small plane. The idea was to lease out the plane and space in the hangar. We'd be able to travel more easily for both business and recreation, and the cost would be covered by the plane and space leases.

My brother called me one day and we started talking about how I viewed things differently than most people. When I told him about the jet and hanger, he asked me how I was going to pull this one off, and I laid out my plan to him. The way I looked at it at that time, I was a failure compared to him. He'd built a house from scratch and put a car in the garage. I'd been in construction all my life and never built a house from the ground up. Now I was basically just building a bigger garage and putting a bigger car in it.

The regional international airport was expanding, and we were working out a contract to lease part of the expansion land to build on. To this day I still can't believe that in the process of hammering out the particulars, the entire project came to a screeching halt because of gopher tortoises. At least that's what they told me. The land was occupied by gopher tortoises, which are a threatened species and the official Florida state reptile. They couldn't be disturbed or relocated.

I tried to come up with every possible option for not disturbing the tortoises, including suspending the hangar so it didn't touch the ground. But the landowners wouldn't budge. In hindsight, I'm glad the deal fell through. The next few years proved to be very challenging both personally and financially, and this would have ended up being just another costly error in judgment.

Not all our real estate purchases were for business purposes. One day I saw an ad for a land grab in Wyoming, so

Nishi and I hopped on a plane to check it out. It was near Fort Laramie, and this place was indescribably beautiful. We bought a forty-acre ranch about three hours from Denver. My buddy Mike flew out and bought some property as well.

Every now and again, I'd fly to Denver and drive to the ranch to watch the sunset over the mountain range. There are two little hills on the property with a seasonal creek running between them that bends around one of the hills.

At night, the stars came out to play, and the air was crisp as a plethora of lights screamed across the vast cosmos. I'd stare out into the deafening silence, the wind cutting through the tree line, picking up dust and swirling it across the plains. The big friggin' mule deer and other animals came out and took up positions for another night of grazing, feeding, and survival. I'd sit there drinking coffee and photographing the stunning beauty of the night.

I've been blessed and tested at many levels of success, but I've never taken it for granted. Experiences throughout my life have taught me that success sometimes leads to failure. But I would soon learn that whatever you can build can be destroyed virtually overnight.

# CHAPTER 10

## The Not-so-Sunshiny State

**Fire, Wind, and Rain**

Growing up in the streets, you knew someone was always getting hustled one way or another. But when you got hustled, you knew what the vig was. I always looked at the "prosti-suits" as lame and somewhat geeky, certainly not willing to get their hands dirty. Now I know why they never get their hands dirty. These guys are the masters of the hustle and taught the gangsters to hustle for them. And they change the vig, the odds, and the rules, all while we're playing their game.

Our first experience with slimy sharks in suits went something like this. We got a call at 3:00 a.m. from the police informing us that one of our duplexes had burned down. In shock, I raced out to the property to be sure no one was injured and that our tenants had someplace to stay for the night. I drove one tenant to a motel, and the other made arrangements to stay with her family. I later named her The Torch.

This tenant had had her utilities shut off for lack of payment. She'd been using candles for light and forgot to blow them all out before she went to bed. One of the candles caught the apartment on fire. I was at home asleep at the time, completely unaware that my tenant had no power. Yet, my insurance company investigated me for arson.

That's not what fazed me, though. When my policy expired, the insurance company canceled every policy on every one of my properties. I'd had the policy less than a year, they had to pay out $70,000 on one claim, and they weren't going to recoup that anytime soon. They decided it was better to cut and run, and that's exactly what they did.

At that time, it was difficult to secure insurance in South Florida because it's in the middle of a storm zone, and even more difficult if you'd just filed a claim. If you have a mortgage on your property, you have to have insurance, or the bank can call your loan. We were left scrambling to cover multiple properties on short notice. No single company would cover them all, so we ended up spreading the liability among multiple companies. I learned a valuable lesson about how insurance companies clearly prioritize their bottom line and not their customers. In hindsight, it turned out to be a great introduction to what was about to happen.

By 2004, after three years of working our asses off renovating, constructing, and organizing a beautiful real estate portfolio of thirty-plus single family, multi-family, and commercial units, we were finally getting a respectable cash flow thanks to lots of sweat equity. We were about to close on a seventy-percent cash-out refinance that would pay off all the small loans and mortgages, leaving us with just one monthly payment. The Plan had us well on our way to financial freedom.

I'd just finished grouting the kitchen floor of our last rental unit and felt really good about getting it done. I remember this unit because it was an old cracker-box-style house with a lemonade porch and columns on the front. I walked out of the house, spread my arms wide, grabbed a column on my right and a column on my left, stretched my back, and let out an exhale I can still feel to this day. I stood there and thought, "I'm done!" Now we could work on the warehouse we'd bought and finally open the brick-oven pizzeria I'd always wanted.

Three weeks later, Hurricane Francis stopped by. Our real estate—our livelihood—was right in her path. The roof of that lemonade porch ripped off the house like a zipper, flew up and over the house, and ended up two football field lengths away. In one motion, the roof of the warehouse that was going to be our pizzeria lifted and fell back down. I lost the entire 4,000 square foot roof, plus the big front plate glass window.

Ten of our buildings suffered everything from torn off roofs to shattered windows (even the ones I'd boarded up) to flooding. One of our duplexes lost both kitchens and all its windows, even though I'd boarded them. In our ten-family building, one tenant left a plate in the sink that covered and completely blocked the drain and had left the faucet open after the water was shut off. When the city finally restored water service, the sink ran for a few hours over the plate-covered drain and flooded four apartments. We did have a bit of luck when a sixty-foot oak tree fell, spanning three backyards, and didn't hit any houses.

Then there was our home, a nicely landscaped house with a fenced-in backyard and pool, all on three-quarters of an acre. Part of the roof ended up in the driveway across the street, and the fence was scattered all over the neighborhood. A tree pierced the side of the in-ground pool, and our electric mast snapped. The city imposed martial law—anyone caught outside between 7:00 p.m. and 7:00 a.m. was arrested, no questions asked—so cleanup and repair time was restricted.

Seeing firsthand the damage done to ten of our investment properties and our home was devastating. But that was just the start. Two weeks later, Hurricane Jeanne finished the job her sister had started. We didn't stick around to see Jeanne in person. We took off to Atlanta with just the clothes on our backs and all our important papers.

What the first hurricane didn't destroy, the second hurricane did. Everything we'd worked our asses off to create was gone. It was worse than starting from zero. Every property we owned was damaged and needed repairs to some extent. We had mortgages to pay on each property, but not necessarily a tenant who could pay their rent. We had no food and no electricity. I sat on my couch for a couple of weeks stoned on Xanax. How could I help anyone else?

There were seven storms that year, some of which required evacuations, and each storm after Francis and Jeanne just added insult to our already injured properties.

## Putting Shit Back Together

We were caught off guard. We never expected to suffer damage that severe to any of our properties. After all, this shit always happens to other people, right? After taking some time feeling sorry for ourselves, we had some serious work to do. Nishi handled the phones and endless reams of paperwork, while I handled the inspections, adjusters, and gutting and cleanup. Sprawled in the streets and in yards was what seemed like endless mounds of plaster, sheetrock, broken windows, shingles, roll roofs, collapsed ceilings, and every other type of building debris you can think of.

In the beginning, nobody could get dumpsters for all the debris, so we located a tow-behind container to haul stuff to the dump. Now we also needed a bigger truck and an enclosed trailer to haul materials in. Nobody had a goddamn tool or any building supplies along the east coast of Florida. Literally. So, we located, ordered, and picked up tools and materials from Atlanta.

I made that haul to and from Atlanta so many times over the next six months, I needed to alter my route. Instead of taking the Florida Turnpike to I-75, I sometimes took I-95 and cut across Georgia to Atlanta from the east. It added an hour to the trip, but it was worth it just so I didn't see the same fucking cows and eat at the same shitty burger joints.

One of my tenants had run into a little bad luck before the hurricanes, so I offered him a job. Ends up that out of all this bullshit, I got tossed a bone. I'm not a religious person, but meeting Dread was a godsend. I didn't know at the time that he would become a member of my extended family. He's proven to be one of the nicest, warmhearted men you could be blessed to call a friend.

When he asked what kind of job he'd be doing, I said, "You're a carpenter and you've been around construction sites your whole life, right? Long hours, shit work, and hopefully paid weekly." He said, "Yes."

We took off running. I'd drop the empty dump container off at one of the houses, then go to the other house, pick up the cargo trailer, and head to Atlanta to get materials. I'd take off in the morning and come back sometime the following night. While I did that, Dread gutted the house, removing damaged sheetrock and everything else that needed to be replaced.

During and immediately after a storm, everybody is neighborly. Until they aren't. It took a while for everyone to get their electricity restored. We were all in the same boat, so everybody was being all friendly, helping each other out. But we had a different problem. During the storm, the power mast on the house got damaged. We couldn't get our power back on at the same time as everybody else because we needed to replace our mast.

For a few weeks, we'd been running a generator night and day, and everyone was cool with that because they were running generators, too. After the neighbors got their electricity back, it was weeks before we could get ours restored. So, we continued using the generator day and night, much to the chagrin of our neighbors who couldn't sleep because it was so loud. And believe me, they bitched and complained every goddamn day.

People can be quite ridiculous, and here's a story that was going around at the time. Apparently, somebody woke up in the middle of the night and heard their generator running, but the air conditioner wasn't working. Going out to check on the generator, he found that someone had stolen it and left a lawnmower engine running in its place. Cruel? Just another part of the neighbor experience.

* * *

## Pants Down and Bend Over

I truly believe the manner in which our insurance claims were handled is how my deep cynicism for the system began. We always prided ourselves on cleaning up properties—painting, tiling, and freshening up the places—providing a clean and renovated unit for the comfort of our tenants. Now we had the (hopefully) once-in-a-lifetime experience of filing twenty separate insurance claims on ten separate properties. What I learned during this whole rebuild and restitution process shocked and appalled me.

The insurance companies didn't answer their phones for the first few days after the first storm, and the adjusters still hadn't come to inspect the damage by the time the second storm hit. The adjusters were dealing with the more severely damaged properties first, and once they started answering calls, most of the insurance companies were giving us a blanket "no" or "wait and see" about our claims. One company told us we didn't even have a policy with them. They finally relented when we showed them all our checks that they'd cashed. Assholes.

I've been involved in construction since my teens, so I understand there's always some shady element working the puppet strings in the background. From the guys in the garbage industry to the guys selling cement, you can find some sleaze every step of the way. Not everybody is involved in bribes and kickbacks, but more than a few are.

I stood in awe at the level of criminal enterprises wearing suits and masquerading as honest bankers and insurance representatives. After all, they have their slick TV commercials advertising how much they care and how they happily provide security and protection to the families with kids and puppies. What they don't show you is what they actually do after a storm or fire as the family is in tears and the insurance adjuster is walking over the dead puppy and calculating whether they actually have to pay for the children's burns. It's all about the dollars, and it definitely makes no sense.

After the storms, some mortgage companies let us skip one payment if our property was damaged, and just added that missed payment onto the end of our loan. I guess this is because they assume we'll be able to get our insurance claim settled and start getting our property back in order within that timeframe. Of course, that didn't happen. The insurance adjusters were inspecting the total losses first, and then getting around to properties that were "just damaged" to make their reports to the insurance companies. While we were waiting in line for inspections, we still had mortgages to pay.

Learning the difference between an Actual Cash Value Policy and a Replacement Cost Policy was the first clue we received in how crooked the insurance racket can be. An Actual Cash Value Policy sounded fine when we bought the insurance. Besides which, it was the only type of policy available in our area at that time, and you've got to have insurance if you've got a mortgage on your property.

With a Replacement Cost Policy, when there's damage to your property you get paid the actual cost of repairing or replacing it, after the deductible. With an Actual Cash Value Policy, which is what we had, you get paid the original cost of the building or materials, less wear and tear. So if the front window of your 1950s-era house broke, you don't get paid the $200 it costs to replace it today, you get paid based on the $30 it cost back in 1950 less the age and condition of the window. After your deductible, you get about $23 to replace that $200 window. Multiply that by thousands of dollars in damage, and you understand why so many property owners just walk away after a major event like a hurricane. Now, this was back in 2004, and I'm sure things have gotten better since then (that's sarcasm).

The next thing we learned was how crooked the banks were. Since your bank has a financial stake in your property as the lien holder, they're listed as an "additional insured" on your insurance policy. Basically, both you and the bank that holds the mortgage are covered in the event of a loss, so the insurance company issues a "double-endorsement" check when they settle the claim. That means both you and your mortgage company must endorse the check in order for it to be cashed.

We endorsed the first check we received and sent it to the mortgage company to endorse so we could deposit the check and start paying for repairs. Only thing is, the mortgage company didn't give us the money. They kept the money until we could prove that the repairs had been made and their inspector had signed off on it. Except, we needed the money to make the repairs. We still had to pay the mortgage, so didn't have cash for the repairs. If you think this was just a onetime fluke, think again. We had twenty separate claims, and it happened over and over.

Here's the third way you get screwed. Now you have to borrow money from a bank to make the repairs, so you can get the money the other bank is sitting on. That's only if you can find a bank willing to give you a loan, which they won't do if the property is gutted and isn't generating any income. Meanwhile, you still have to keep paying your mortgage. This is the point where you go to friends and family with hat in hand and offer to pay them higher interest than cash in the bank, or just walk away.

How many properties did we walk away from? None. We kept paying mortgages and making repairs as some money started coming in from the insurance claims. There were endless sleepless nights staring at the water-logged ceiling of our home, and I felt pains in my chest daily. We needed a way out of this mess, and fast.

I can't completely trash the whole insurance industry. There were some people who came out and helped us. We got paid on about twenty percent of our claims within a few months of the adjusters inspecting and making their report. The rest of the claims took almost two years, time and money that we'd never get back.

The delays created almost as much damage as the hurricanes, with about three other strong storms adding insult to injury. If half of a ceiling had fallen in originally, we'd get paid for about a quarter of the repair cost after the deductible. But the roof was exposed because no one had tarps, so the entire ceiling would have to be replaced because of water damage and mold.

I can't begin to calculate how much we lost in tangible assets from our retirement plan, in addition to loss of equity (both sweat and financial) and the staggering cost of making repairs not paid for by the insurance companies.

My friends all told me not to do it, but we sold every single property we owned in Florida. I put them on the market and ran manic hustle classified ads like "Crazy Craig's prices won't be beat" and "The sun is out, and the clowns are cutting deals." The ads were stupid but effective. Houses I'd bought for $30k in $100k neighborhoods now sold for $90k. We were looking for a fresh start, and Atlanta was where we were going to find it.

But moving to Atlanta wasn't the biggest change we'd experience. While still in Florida, we found out that Nishi was pregnant. We were living in our hurricane-damaged house, lying in bed every night staring up at the water-stained ceiling, making plans to get out of the post-hurricane mess. While I was hustling to sell our properties, we moved into an apartment, so our baby could be brought home to someplace that wasn't falling apart.

People say having a child changes you in ways you can't imagine, and I was ready for that kind of personal, deep-in-your-soul change. You want everything to be okay in your life before you have kids, even if that isn't actually possible. At that point in my life, I was a spoiled, sarcastic, cynical, cocky prick.

At the same time, I was forty-ish, struggling with midlife, and barely keeping my head above water mentally. I had to make some significant changes. I decided I wasn't playing other people's games and I wasn't putting up with anyone else's bullshit. I had a mini-me on the way, and daddy wasn't going to be anybody's bitch anymore – not to the bankers, or the lawyers, or the insurance companies. Hearing family members talk about their kids and how they'd altered their lives, I was ready to share that experience.

I know everyone is supposed to say it, but I really mean it when I say my daughter's birth was the best thing that ever happened to me. Some say that fathers shouldn't watch the birth of their children, but I think that's stupid. Despite the challenges of labor and delivery, it was the most amazing thing I've ever seen. And it created a bond between Nishi and me and our daughter like nothing I could have ever imagined.

Of course, you can't have a kid and not have a birth story. It's rough watching someone you love go through that type of pain, and I did my best to distract Nishi and help her relax. When the doctor and I cracked jokes about how hard it was delivering a baby, she was not amused. This woman with a heart of gold, the love of my life, looked at me like she wanted me dead.

I somewhat redeemed myself by asking the nurse if my wife could have the epidural she'd been waiting for. Nishi's eyes lit up like I'd brought her a fancy box of chocolates. The nursed asked her if she wanted an epidural, and she said yes (duh). Then the nurse said, "Okay, fill out this form and sign the waiver." I just about lost my shit. We'd done the preliminary check-in the week before, so we wouldn't have to deal with paperwork in the middle of delivery. What a ridiculous system, fucking with someone who's in pain like that. But that day I finally met the person whose voice had been in my head since Jamaica.

Here I was, once again on the brink of a new adventure, this time with a little one in tow. This time we'd do it differently. I'd have to be someone I didn't know, and I wasn't sure if I could be. We'd have to find a different way of doing business, a way that reduced the chances of getting fucked over like we had been before and creating our livelihood on our own terms.

# CHAPTER 11

## Georgia

**A New Start, a New Person, a New Passion**

We'd made so many trips to Georgia buying materials and tools for the hurricane cleanup that we really started liking the Atlanta area. Already in the process of selling off all our Florida properties, we settled on a beautiful brick four-bedroom Colonial house in Lilburn. It needed some work, but what the hell was a little more sweat equity?

We figured we'd start out our Georgia business dealings slowly. I'm laughing here, because by the time we actually moved, we already had our house, Dread's house, the ranch in Wyoming, and an office condo in an Atlanta building where all the local real estate gurus held their monthly meetings. Connecting with big investors would be like shooting fish in a barrel. We paid ninety-five grand for the place that had sold for two-seventy-five two years earlier, and we renovated it. Taking it slow just is not in our DNA.

Nishi and I were both burned out from all the insurance bullshit, restoring damaged properties, selling those properties, and finally moving. And we had a brand-new baby. After settling into our new home, we decided to take a break and head down to Cancún. My niece had been staying with us to help with the baby, so we brought her along. We stayed at one of those all-inclusive joints and just hung out enjoying the beach and each other.

In our exploration of the area, we stumbled upon a real estate company selling some beachfront property in Sisal, a beautiful, quiet little town across the peninsula in the Yucatán. It was our last day in Cancún, so we extended our stay to go check out this property. We left the baby with my niece for the day and told her that if anything happened to us, the kid was hers (she was slightly freaked out by this). I made a bunch of calls to be sure my attorney in the States knew what was going on and what arrangements we wanted made.

The real estate company flew us over on a private plane. The pilot made sure to "wow" us by flying over the pyramid at Chichen Itza. We landed in Mérida, forty minutes from Sisal, and after exploring the city for a couple of hours, we fell in love with the culture and warmth of the people. We bought a beachfront lot in Sisal, hoping to build a house and move there in the near future.

Back home, we were getting a reputation in the real estate industry and started going to real estate shows and doing radio interviews. I realized that my true passion is teaching people about financial literacy and how to be your own bank. But everyone and their mother was now in real estate, and people who didn't know anything about the business were making hundreds of thousands of dollars on transactions. With very little experience, people were getting lucky on some deals, but ultimately setting themselves up for disaster long-term.

At these real estate expos, I talked to people who'd studied finance and economics in school but knew nothing about the real world of money (commodities) and currency (paper and electronic assets). After just a few minutes of discussion, they told me they were never taught about money. All those student loans for a degree that might not even get you a good job. Even if it did, why work for someone else?

I got this idea for a website where people could find commercial and residential investment properties—a database of owner-financed, lease-options, rent-to-owns, and other creative financing properties. People could buy, sell, or trade properties and set up their own transactions, and we'd get a small vig just for the listing. We'd go to all the real estate trade shows to advertise the site and, eventually, we could add businesses to it. At the time, we were one of the first on the web.

I had a buddy who was a computer wiz. His family had put us up in their house during our frequent visits to Atlanta, and we'd become close. I asked Max if he could build the website, and he said yes. That was the start of our website business venture.

We spent a small fortune building and promoting our website. My goal was to spread financial literacy to as many people as possible. Here we had a great tool – an easy step-by-step website at your fingertips to help you through the process. But it all fell on deaf ears. I couldn't understand why people didn't want to learn about the onslaught that would soon befall them. Our motto was "Mind your own business. If not, someone else will."

* * *

## The Beginning of Infamy

My stomach churned with butterflies, I wanted to vomit, and I thought I was going to crap my pants. I could feel the excitement in the room as everyone listened to the speaker on stage but sweat poured down my face and my palms were wet. Then came the announcement.

"Up next, Craig Sotkovsky is here to talk about his newly formed company, a website that pulls together everything you need for real estate investment. With over twenty years in the real estate and construction industry, Mr. Sotkovsky will give you the edge in owner-financed properties, lease options, note creation, and creative real estate financing." Speaking at the Gaylord Palms Resort real estate expo was a big deal for me. Now the pressure was on.

I hadn't spoken in public in years, but I thought the weeks of practicing with Nishi would be enough to get back into it. I was wrong. My heart was pounding, the room was getting smaller, and my tie was cutting off oxygen to my brain. Pulling myself together, I thought, "I've got this." There were only a couple dozen people seated facing the stage, the rest all milling around the room "networking."

I grabbed the microphone, turned to face the audience, and said, "Hi, I'm Craig." Before I could say another word, the mic screeched and everyone in the expo hall turned to stare at me. Hundreds of faces. I was supposed to talk for a half hour, but all I could remember of my speech was a brief introduction of my company. I lasted five minutes, but it felt like hours.

Shortly after this debacle, a guy approached my booth and asked about my company and its spokesperson. That would be me. He grabbed me and said, "Okay, if you're the one I have to work with, just follow my lead." Within the hour I was on his radio show, and then there was no stopping me. After the expo, I hit Atlanta, Los Angeles, Miami, Memphis, Philadelphia, and New York City promoting my website company and telling people about creative financing.

I've been speaking publicly now for almost ten years. I've been on dozens of radio shows and talked to tens of thousands of people since the Gaylord Palms. It's been a lot of fun, a huge learning experience, but sometimes frustrating. People are often stunned to find out you can finance real estate with credit cards, credit lines, and personal note creation, and many of them just don't want to believe it. Some said what I was promoting was robbing people. I laughed at that.

Once we sat them down and showed them the whole process and that they would never miss another investment opportunity, their jaws dropped. I was like a kid in a candy store, obsessed with wealth creation and showing off how smart I was. It was the Wild West in real estate, an anything-goes attitude toward mortgages and financing, the crazy calm before the shitstorm that nearly destroyed our economy. Funny thing is, we're right in the same place now, the part leading up to the bubble bursting. All the signs are there, but few people want to see it.

※ ※ ※

**The Expo and Exposure**

By this time, I was traveling like a madman and it was really stressful for my family back home, as well as for me. Looking at my upcoming schedule, I couldn't believe the next few weeks. There was a real estate show in Atlanta, then I was driving to New York City for the Real Estate Expo at the Hotel Pennsylvania. Then a three-day publicity summit the following weekend that I fought relentlessly to get into. The week after that, I'd be back in Atlanta for an Anthony Robbins event.

The real estate show in Atlanta was the last monthly show to be held in my office building. The manager of our building and several others around Atlanta "borrowed" a few hundred million dollars and rapidly relocated overseas with the funds. The management office was in the lobby of our building, so the Feds, State Troopers and local cops were in the building almost daily. Condo owners were asking about the fate of their office units because the building was behind in its utility payments. I got antsy as owners tried to sell their units and got no bites at all. Who wants to buy a unit in a building that was ready to close its doors? I'd paid close to $100k for my office, and I could see the shitstorm brewing.

At the same time, it became clear that the website business was not working. Things didn't go quite as I'd planned. It turned out Max and I didn't work well together. Personally, I loved the guy, but that's not necessarily a healthy foundation for a great business venture.

After four years of trying to get the thing off the ground, the markets were changing rapidly. We needed to change along with them, but I didn't know how. It was time to cut our losses and get out. I formulated a plan to put an end to the business. Being who I am, I chose to bow out graciously by taking the brunt of the financial losses. I didn't realize how messed up things had gotten until Nishi and I went through all the paperwork to wrap up the financials.

I learned a lot about the magic money industry. Internet businesses were pretty new at the time, and we figured out too late that without traffic to your site, you're dead in the water. With all the seminars Max and I attended, I thought all our bases were covered, but they weren't. I dropped the ball by not checking his work, and I was now at another major crossroad in my life.

Between the debacle with the office building and the imminent failure of the website venture, I really needed the distraction of the upcoming New York Real Estate Expo. It's always good going back home, and my buddy Mike – who always has my back – was flying up from Florida to help out. But New York turned out to be where everything I'd been doing on the road for the past year-and-a-half came to a screeching halt.

The expo was the same traveling circus it always was, and probably always will be. The guy hawking land sales on his private island off Belize, the biggest sharks in real estate history showing people how to make money flipping houses, and people selling exotic timeshares (that you'd probably only use twice in your life) for $20,000.

This time, I was invited to sit in on a roundtable discussion about financing real estate purchases and renovations using credit cards and credit lines. I was an expert at buying properties this way, then either selling or refinancing to pay back the credit cards. We'd done this a few dozen times and showed people how to use constructive debt to get ahead instead of destructive debt buying useless shit like overpriced vehicles and big-screen TVs.

※ ※ ※

**Publicity, Transition, and Realization**
As the expo was wrapping up, I had a few days to prepare for the upcoming publicity summit. I didn't know what to expect but hoped it would be a positive change. I teleconferenced with the summit's prep team and was one of about a hundred participants from around the world. We were all the best of the best in our respective fields, handpicked through an application and interview process, all of which came with a vig. We interviewed for the chance to appear on the morning shows, radio shows, magazines, and for the newly exploding online publications. Everyone else had written a book and were experts in their field, and I was wondering what the fuck I was doing there. Now the fun began.

They say that when the student is ready, the teacher will appear. People started checking into the hotel on Wednesday, and I quickly found some inspiring people. I met a woman from

Washington, D.C. who had no arms. She came alone but somehow managed to change her outfits between meetings. I also met "Jaws" from the James Bond films, a huge man with a heart of gold.

Each participant had about thirty seconds (a basic elevator pitch) to impress and convince an outlet to put us on their television or radio show or in their magazine. My pitch was creating financial independence through time and money management. In my world, money means you, your time and labor, relationships, and physical commodities such as salt, rice, grains, gold, silver, and fruits and vegetables. I wanted to show people how each family can be a corporation and how to create financial freedom, so you can spend more money (time) with your family and friends.

To my surprise, I was turned down by all the mainstream media outlets and was laughed at for wanting to teach people how to become their own bank. But I was picked up by the alternative news outlets, and over time I became one of the most sought-after people for teaching the difference between money and currency. Those that control the currency all belong to a worldwide club that the average person earning a wage will never get to join. I wanted to help people escape the prison of mortgage payments, car payments, medical bills, education costs, and being taxed to death (the government's vig).

For me, the morning session was a bust. I was getting used to hearing "No way," and my defeated attitude was written all over my face. When the afternoon session started, while everyone else was back at it in the ballroom, I just sat in the hallway trying to clear my head.

Out of nowhere, a guy sat next to me and asked why I wasn't in the other room giving my pitch. I turned and came face-to-face with Kurek Ashley, one of the best peak performance minds in the world. (His internationally best-selling book *How Would Love Respond?* is a must-read.) After about forty minutes of sharing stories and some uplifting thoughts, he'd gotten me back in the game. "No" became "Call me," and "Maybe" became "What's your schedule like?"

The experience solidified for me that I should shut down the website business. Some of the sharpest business and marketing minds were telling me we needed to make some changes to the website. So, I changed my pitch from promoting the website business to promoting myself.

After the publicity summit, I headed back to Atlanta for the Anthony Robbins seminar. It was a great couple of days with all the motivation, inspiration, and talks to put ourselves into peak performance. The firewalk, walking barefoot across a bed of hot coals, was one of the best metaphors I'd found for life. I'd always been into self-meditation and, at times, self-medication, but meditation always won out. I learned from my time in Jamaica and all the mind control seminars I'd attended, that you can do whatever you set your mind to. I was now willing to take on a new mindset and change the course of my life. I then had a few experiences that showed me I was on the right path.

## It's All About the People

One of my favorite places to go in the Atlanta area is a Korean spa in Duluth. I go there when I need a massage and some time in the steam room and sauna. Afterward, I often grab a coffee at the shop on the corner to take home with me.

On one particular day, I noticed a man sitting by himself at an outside table. It was clear he'd been there for some time because his ashtray was overflowing, and he looked drawn and nervous. I just couldn't stop staring at him as I walked in, and I continued to watch him chain smoke through the big front window as I waited for my coffee.

When I walked out of the shop, I felt compelled to sit down with him. I pulled up a chair and helped myself to one of his cigarettes, figuring that would probably snap him out of his obviously distressed thoughts. I apologized and introduced myself, and he responded with "It's nice to meet you." He said his name was Kim.

I asked him what he was doing, and he said he'd been sitting there for about an hour deciding on his next move. I told him I'd sat down because I'd seen the desperation in his face, and he smiled with relief.

We talked about our families and our kids and eventually got around to talking about our businesses. His had recently failed, he was faced with losing his home and his vehicles, and no one in his family knew about it yet. He felt he had shamed his family and that they would lose all respect for him when they found out.

I talked to him about my life – as a kid in the construction industry, 9/11, the hurricanes and insurance nightmare, and my latest business fuckup. I encouraged him to sit down with his family and explain the situation. But in his culture, he told me, it's easier to just end your life, and that's what he was debating while sitting at that table chain smoking.

I told him that if he did that, he would affect many lives in a profoundly terrible way. His children would grow up without a loving, strong father who can admit his failures and move on to the next success. I told him my greatest successes were becoming a husband and a father. He looked at me like I had six heads, but he welcomed the encouragement. After about an hour of conversation, I could hear the relief in his voice and see it in his body language. He was comfortable with his new friend, and he had made a decision.

He asked me to go with him to his car, which I did. He opened the door, reached in, and pulled out a .38, which he gently handed to me. I removed the bullets and gave it back to him. He cried as he thanked me, and said he was going to talk to his family. After that, I called Nishi and went home. I never saw Kim again.

For a few months after that, I paid closer attention to the news to see if a suicide popped up, but nothing did. I hoped my newfound friend took whatever lesson he needed from that night and created a beautiful life with his family and friends. Paths cross for a reason, and Kim gave me insight into the importance of getting your head in the right space.

I was attending a lot of real estate conference breakfasts in the Atlanta area to promote the company. There were all the usual speakers and mentors sharing their knowledge of current industry trends, but I loved meeting the new investors, the ones who were just getting started. Their eyes lit up when I talked to them about making money in real estate through non-traditional means.

One of these meetings was at an old hotel, part of a chain, with a tacky chandelier in the lobby and Art Deco décor. They were providing the typical morning buffet – shitty bagels, coffee, congealed scrambled eggs, and bacon glued together fresh from the microwave. It was an early morning meeting filled with guys trying to give up their nine-to-five jobs by hustling real estate, determined to succeed by any means necessary. The sooner they learned the tricks of the game, the quicker the steak went on their family's table.

The room was filled with all kinds of guys, wearing everything from contractor pants with tape measures on their belts, to khakis and polo shirts. I was there to meet a young kid named Mel, whom I'd met at a previous conference, to promote my online company.

I noticed another young guy that seemed out of place. He was tall and good-looking, wearing a suit that was a bit too big for his lanky frame. He seemed very nervous, but also sure of himself, and looked starry-eyed and hungry.

As the meeting began, I sat across from Mel. We were talking about the other guys in the room when the suited kid sat down next to Mel, who introduced him as his buddy Eamon.

Before the two main real estate guys went on stage, the speaker introduced everyone in the room. One by one, everybody stood up and made their pitch like it was a Narcotics Anonymous meeting. At least, that's what it reminded me of. In the meantime, cards were being passed back and forth with guys talking and trying to cut deals between yawns. Just another typical, unremarkable early morning real estate conference.

As weeks passed, Mel sort of faded into the background, but I saw more and more of Eamon. He came to my house to talk about things he'd need to break into the industry. Most newbie investors come to the table thinking anything is possible until they realized the industry, especially in Atlanta, is overrun with fraud. But Eamon seemed to take it in stride.

He would call me, or we'd meet at my office or home, and our conversations quickly went from professional to personal. Mentoring him was a joy because I learned so much from him. We'd joke that he could sell just about anything, and he was bold and ready to take on the world.

* * *

## The Olympian and the Stretch Master

My next experience was something I didn't know was possible...the healing of very old physical wounds. My buddy Mike turned me on to Gebi, one of the best Olympic kite surfers in the world. Mike had been working out with him and told me I should drive down to Fort Pierce to see this guy.

By this time, I was thinking a lot about how I needed a change in my life, so one morning I jumped in the car and made the drive. At this point, I felt like ten pounds of shit in a five-pound bag. I was a mess physically, mentally, emotionally, and spiritually.

When I got to my destination, I met Gebi and got my body stretched. And I mean stretched in a way I didn't know was possible. After about twenty minutes of Gebi pulling and pushing, he told me to hold on while he called his friend and trainer, Bob Cooley. I only heard a little of the conversation, mostly Gebi describing this obese, out-of-shape guy with a completely fucked up knee. Gebi passed me the phone, and this total stranger described exactly what was wrong with me; my jacked-up hamstrings were messing with my knee. I was in awe.

A few minutes later, I was driving back to Atlanta to pick up some clothes, and then on to Virginia for a symposium my new friend Bob was having. All I had to do was fly Gebi there, and I could sit in. I was all in for this one.

The symposium was held in someone's house and, honestly, it looked like some New Age granola shit was about to happen. People from all walks of life were there, but they all had one thing in common; they were fit and trim and obviously healthy. Then there was me, the sore thumb of the group, dreaming of cheeseburgers and chocolate shakes.

But I was willing to try anything to get myself and my life straightened out, and I'm glad I did. I was put on a stretch board and pulled and pushed and stretched in ways that made me feel transformed. In that one weekend, Bob became one of my heroes. Not only did he fix what doctors couldn't in twenty years, but he also took my mind in a different direction and straightened out something that had hindered my ability to move forward in my life.

I can't tell you how excited I was to be feeling muscle pain around my knee, instead of the bone pain I'd suffered with for decades. After that weekend, I continued to practice the stretching exercises I'd learned and felt real improvements, both physically and mentally. The more I improved, the better I felt about myself. I'd gained two very important people in my life, Bob Cooley and Michael Gebhart.

About a year later, Bob invited me to another stretching session, this one at a media mogul's lake house outside of Atlanta. I jumped at the chance and again was stretched beyond what I thought my limits were, mentally and physically. I highly recommend Bob's book *The Genius of Flexibility*. It changed my life, and if you're in pain it can change yours as well.

Sometimes we don't recognize some of the most influential, inspirational, impactful people in our lives until we've been a cocky, know-it-all ass for a few decades. My dad was one of these influencers in my life, always ready to share his pure wisdom born from experience. Of course, as a kid, teen, and young adult, I knew everything and brushed him off. Thankfully, I absorb things like a sponge and now still remember his stories. One in particular has stayed with me all these years.

During his time in Korea, my dad and his unit were trekking through a hilly area of the country. The summit they had to climb to get to their destination was quite a challenge. Just as they reached the top, they saw they had to climb another peak beyond that, and that peak was no easy task, either. As the day wore on, they kept climbing and climbing, one peak after another.

Finally, they were told that the top was fast approaching. The end was near. They were almost done climbing. They continued climbing, exhausted and relieved. They made it to the very top of the last peak, only to find another one above that. I remember my father's face as he told this story. At that point of the climb, he said, he felt defeated and tears rolled down his face.

I often think of this story when I'm feeling exhausted and everything seems to be going wrong. It helps me find a way to do what he did – take a knee, wipe the tears away, and keep going.

✳ ✳ ✳

### Here Comes the Crash, and It's Time to Go

One night, I was sitting around with some friends talking about how the credit markets were drying up. One of them, Big T, said, "You know the banks are changing rates right in front of people's eyes, and they don't even know about it." His wife and I laughed and said he didn't know what the hell he was talking about. He's a very practical and financially conservative guy. His wife and I think like entrepreneurs and fly by the seat of our pants. So, I asked him what proof he had.

You know those legals you get with your credit card bill? All that fine print in legalese that the rest of us toss in the trash without even glancing at? Well, he actually read them all the way through. I was more impressed that he'd read it than what he told me was in them.

Basically, they were changing the rules of the game while the rest of us were all distracted by something else (they still are and most of us still are). In what other industry can two parties enter into a contract, and only one of them can change the terms without the consent of the other? That's craziness, but it happens every day. Just read the small print on your next bill.

At that time, we were getting screwed by the banks. I had so many credit cards without balances (I was, after all, a deadbeat), that they retracted my credit lines, which messed with my credit rating and ability to jump on opportunities. It was another shit show.

On top of that, I lost three-quarters of a million dollars when the company behind a high-yield investment opportunity folded. When these "qualified investments" go under, you only get pennies for every dollar you'd put in. All the markets were rigged, and again the small schmuck was getting screwed.

The final straw was when our neighbor decided to sell his house for half its value, messing with everyone else's home values. I'd had enough. I had my "fuck it" moment and started preparing to move to Mexico.

Part of that preparation was holding about thirteen garage sales. I'd spent tens of thousands of dollars on all this stuff that I was now selling off for pennies on the dollar. Talk about reacting instead of responding. Week after week it was "sell this, sell that" and call after call after call from people wanting to buy tools or dressers or TVs. It felt like an endless task. I reached out to Eamon to see if he knew some people who wanted shit cheap.

It's quite humbling selling off all the things you put so much thought and money into because you thought it would bring you happiness. Now it's bringing you a couple of bucks. Toward the end, I was literally giving stuff away for free. Another putz moment in the onslaught of putz moments. I wondered how I got caught up in so much drama again. I was a hotshot who committed the ultimate sin...believing my own headlines.

Eamon had a buddy Ralph who needed some of the good stuff we had, but he was light on cash and he couldn't pick it up. So, we delivered the furniture right to his doorstep in Atlanta, and it felt really good helping out. There was something fulfilling about unburdening ourselves of all the "stuff" we'd accumulated and giving it to someone who could use it.

A week or two later, Eamon called me, clearly upset, and came over to the house. When he pulled up in his truck, he was crying inconsolably. He'd just found out that Ralph was killed the day before in a car accident. It was a hard thing watching this young man, whom I love, go through this heart-wrenching grief. That situation brought us even closer together. He's still in my life today, and I get such joy from watching him and his wife raise their children. He's always in my thoughts.

In addition to the craziness of trying to get rid of most of our stuff, I was making trips back and forth from Atlanta to Mérida to get everything set up. We needed a house, as well as a retail space because we planned to open a restaurant. I found a great deal in a good location for the store, and a nice furnished rental house through a gringo I'd met. The house was clean and had an office/shop in the back. The store was going to need some fixing up, but it would be a welcomed project. I was already collecting the equipment we needed for the restaurant, and stored the two refrigerators, two stoves, grill, deep fryer, and oven in the living room of the house.

I took a trailer-load of stuff to store at my family's house in New Jersey, and then reloaded and drove the trailer to

Panama City, Florida to be shipped to the port in Progreso. Three weeks after securing our new home, my family and I were on a flight to the Yucatán. The flight was uneventful, and we breezed through customs, but couldn't get my dog until the next day. After a long, tiring day, we caught a cab to the house, walked in, and the master bathroom was covered in hundreds of these little flies that came up through the shower drain – a sure sign of bad plumbing. Needless to say, we were not pleased.

    Over the next few days, we found more issues with the house. Our trailer would be clearing customs any day, so we needed to find a new place to live quickly. I managed to find another house about a block away. I was surprised we could find and secure another house so quickly. When we picked up the trailer, we moved into the new place and never looked back.

# A MEXICAN EPILOGUE

**My Awakening, and Mexico on the Horizon**

Packing up and moving to Mexico may seem like an extreme reaction to yet another financial setback. Most people do that – they react to circumstances instead of responding, just as I did for decades. But this last debacle came along just as I was forming a new realization and new outlook.

In this wonderful country of ours, the system is set up for you to fail. The average person can far too easily slip up and lose everything. Sometimes, like in my case, they fail and lose everything numerous times throughout their lives. There are so many rules and laws controlling every aspect of your life, even the most diligent person is probably breaking a few here and there. Those laws are written to benefit the people who write them or pay someone else to write them, not the rest of us. Follow the money, and you'll eventually find out who's benefitting.

Most people don't realize that you don't actually own anything. Everything you think is yours can be taken away from you in a heartbeat. Someone can slip and fall on your property, and they take everything you've got in a lawsuit. You can lose your job because the CEO of your company decides he's not getting a big enough bonus and the shareholders aren't getting rich fast enough. You get behind on your mortgage, and the bank kicks you out. You spend decades building up a retirement fund, and it disappears during the next economic crash. Even if you manage to avoid these types of catastrophes, you keep getting squeezed tighter and tighter between a paycheck that stays stagnant while the price of basic goods and services keep getting jacked up year after year. And, of course, there are the credit companies standing by to help you stay afloat by getting you so far into destructive debt you'll never get out at thirty percent interest.

Are we all doomed to be slaves to a deeply manipulated system our entire lives? Are we destined to continue being crushed by a global economy designed to enrich the top ten percent at the cost of everyone else? I don't think so. The world is built on words. We're accustomed to being sold a bundle of words through the world of advertising. Some have sought to challenge that world through words on the internet, with varying degrees of success.

Our move to Mexico was all about my daughter. Did I really want her to grow up running on the same hamster wheel I'd spent my life on? I think about everything I've done in my fifty-two years. I can't count how many construction projects I've worked on or owned. I've been party to so many lawsuits and failed endeavors that I stopped counting. Things I've possessed have spanned cities, counties, states and countries. I've eaten through my emotions. I've had the office in the sky overlooking the traffic of a million cars a day. I've been called

Craig, Asshole, and Mr. Sotkovsky. I've imported and exported my life at least a dozen times. I've walked the talk my entire life, mostly in tears. I've self-sabotaged and self-destructed and left other people holding the bag. I've been loathed, mocked and ridiculed, as well as praised, for my thoughts. My reactions to life have been questioned many times. I've lived my life as I saw fit, mostly for experiences and knowledge. I've projected incomes and karma brought the outcomes. I've stood on the shoulders of Titans and have bowed so others could rise. I've loved and lost and lusted and yearned.

How did the move to Mexico turn out? As with most other moves in my life, it was an adventure with lots of good stuff along with the not-so-good stuff. Our restaurant opening was a hit in the community. I met someone who had seen me speak years before and said I'd helped change her life for the better. The beach property turned out to be a mosquito-infested scam. And eventually, we returned to Georgia.

What's next? Stay tuned to find out.

※ ※ ※

At print date, Bitcoin is $6,941.27 and silver is $16.65. And the derivative market is in the multi-quadrillions.

### KEEP STACKING

Made in the USA
Middletown, DE
17 June 2018